The Pioneer
and th
Prairie Lawyer

D0001166

Boone and Lincoln Family Heritage

Biographical and Historical

1603 – 1985

by

Willard Mounts
Denver, Colorado

Printed
by
Johnson Printing Co.
Boulder, Colorado

Cover Art
by
J. Attebery-Lewis
Denver, Colorado

Photographs & Maps by Willard Mounts

Published
by

Ginwill Publishing Company
Denver, Colorado

Published by Ginwill Publishing Company
2585 S. Holly Place, Denver, Colorado

Published 1992 February 12, 1992 (Lincoln's birthday)

Printed in the United States of America on acid free paper
95 94 93   8 7 6

Cover design by J. Attebery-Lewis, Denver, Colorado

Library of Congress Cataloging in Publication Data 91-72847

Mounts, Willard, 1915 -

  Biographical and historical account of Boone and Lincoln families
  Includes index and photographic plates

  1. History   I. The Pioneer and the Prairie Lawyer

  Library of Congress Card Catalog Number 91-72847

ISBN 0-9630038-1-X

Table of Contents

Preface

The purpose in writing this book about the Boones and Lincolns is to bring into focus the close relationships between the two families. Literally hundreds of book have been written about the subjects, but no attempts have been made to follow them through the years in their migrations and interfamily marriages. Others also failed to compare the many similarities between Daniel and Abe, including:

Their forefathers came from England and were of the Quaker faith.

The families migrated together for many years.

There were many marriages between the families throughout the years.

Daniel had no schooling and Abe had less than one year.

At times during their lives, both men lived off the land by farming.

Each built his own log cabin home.

They were experts at handling an ax.

Both had great endurance and could walk many miles without tiring.

Each operated a general store/tavern.

Both were surveyors.

Both enlisted in the state militia and were promoted to captain.

They were state legislators.

Both were referees, arbitrators and judges.

They were honest men and pioneers in their fields.

Both were kind and gentle. Each befriended an aged Indian who was found in a desperate situation along the trail.

Each was quite religious, but neither joined a church.

Each married only once.

Both were reinterred.

Daniel's wife Becky's relatives, the Bryans, were Tory sympathizers and not in favor of rebellion by the Colonists. Abe's wife, Mary, had brothers fighting for the Confederacy.

Abraham Lincoln and Daniel Boone were both elected to the Hall of Fame for Great Americans. Lincoln in 1900 and Boone in 1915.

Introduction

This book covers the Daniel Boone and Abraham Lincoln families from 1603 through 1985 and touches on other historical events of the time that affected their lives, such as wars, inventions and discoveries.

Dedication

To show my gratitude, I dedicate this book to my wife, Ginnie. Without her great help and patience, this book could not have been written.

With much love,
Your husband

Illustrations

1. Map of England
2. Samuel Lincoln home, Hingham, MA
3. Old Ship Church, Hingham, MA
4. Sarah Morgan (mother of Daniel Boone) home, N. Wales, PA
5. Gwynedd Friends Monthly Meeting House, N. Wales, PA
6. Mordecai Lincoln, Sr., home, Scituate, MA
7. Mordecai Lincoln, Sr., gristmill, Scituate, MA
8. Mordecai Lincoln, Jr., ironworks factory, Clarksburg, NJ
9. Mordecai Lincoln, Jr., home, Amity, Berks County, PA
10. Daniel Boone Homestead, Exeter Township, Berks County, PA
11. Exeter Friends Meeting House, Berks County, PA
12. Jacob Lincoln home, Shenandoah Valley, Linville Creek, VA
13. "Virginia John" Lincoln gravestone, Rockingham County, VA
14. Map of Boone-Lincoln migrations
15. Boone Cave, Yadkin River near Mocksville, NC
16. Squire Boone cabin, Daniel Boone State Park, NC
17. Squire & Sarah Morgan Boone tombstone, Joppa Cemetery, NC
18. Cumberland Gap
19. Daniel Boone portrait
20. Fort Harrod, first Kentucky settlement, near Harrodsburg
21. Historic Marker, Point Pleasant, WV
22. Map of Wilderness Trail--Boone-Lincoln country, KY
23. Fort Boonesborough, overlooking Kentucky River
24. Map of Boone-Lincoln country
25. Map of rivers in eastern and central Kentucky
26. Nancy Hanks birthplace, Mikes Run, Antioch, WV
27. Captain Abraham Lincoln marker, Long Run, KY
28. Last Daniel Boone cabin in Kentucky, near Blue Licks
29. Judgment Tree, Femme Osage District, near Definance, MO
30. Schoolhouse, St. Charles County, near Defiance, MO
31. Thomas Lincoln Nall Farm home, near Elizabethtown, KY
32. Richard and Rachel Berry home, Beech Fork, Beechland, KY
33. Abraham Lincoln's birthplace - Cartoon
34. Abraham Lincoln birthplace cabin, Hodgenville, KY

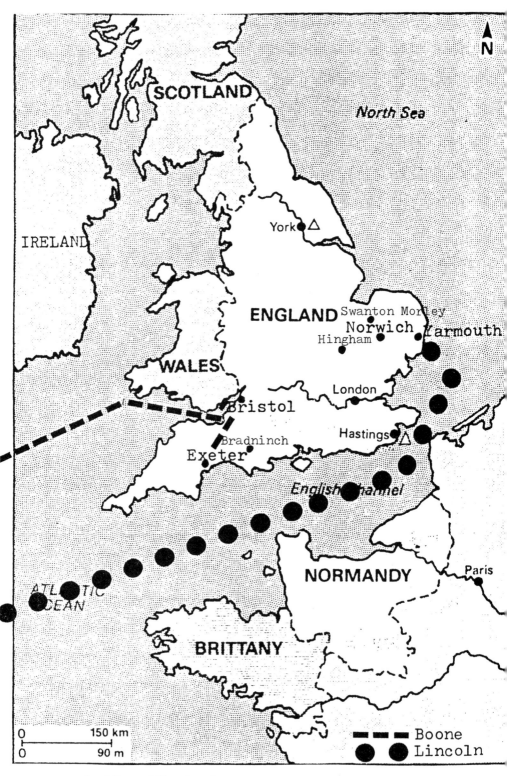

1. *Map of England*
   Swanton Morley – Birthplace of Richard Lincoln
   Bradninch – Home of George Boone

Chapter 1
England (1603)
Dissenters Avoid Persecution
Seek Religious Freedom in America

The ancestors of Daniel Boone and Abraham Lincoln faced suppression and danger in England in the 1600s. Little did they know of the new but different hardships and dangers--and greatness--their migration to America would bring to their families.

The stage for the migrations was set by a proclamation from the Royal Castle declaring, "All those who do not conform to the strict regulations of the Anglican Church will be harried out of the land."

Under such cruel and oppressive mandates, life had become insufferable for those known as Separatists. During the reigns of King James I (1603-25) and King Charles I (1625-49), dissenting groups were severely persecuted by the monarchs through savage coercion and torture. Ears were cut off, nostrils slashed and property confiscated to force people to accept the Anglican faith, the established church of the land. Many were hanged for defying the King's decree. Everyone was expected to worship according to the church's rigid forms and only its members were permitted to participate in political activities.

The dissenters demanded a separation of church and state and the right to worship in their own way. Several dissenting groups, including the Pilgrims, the Puritans and the Religious Society of Friends (Quakers), were becoming established in England during this time, despite the persecutions.

The Quakers believed everyone was created equal in the sight of God and they disobeyed any law they thought unjust, even to the point of refusing to remove their hats to anyone of authority. They also believed that God spoke directly to them in silence and, therefore, felt it was unnecessary to have a minister or priest to perform any ceremonies.

Many Quaker members, along with their organizer and leader, George Fox, were periodically lashed as they were dragged through the streets and thrown into prison.

For the next hundred years or so, dissenting groups left England for America in search of religious freedom. In this migration, the Boone and Lincoln families, both of the Quaker faith, left southern England for new homes across the Atlantic.

Samuel Lincoln (1619-90), Abraham Lincoln's grandfather six generations removed, became an apprentice at age eighteen to Francis Laws, a master weaver. In 1637, they left Norwich in Norfolk County, England, sailing from Yarmouth across the rough Atlantic and migrating to Hingham, Massachusetts. They arrived just seventeen years after the Pilgrims had landed at Plymouth.

Samuel lived a fruitful life. He became successful as a weaver and mariner and also established his own ironworks. He died in 1690, after having raised a large family, and was buried in the cemetery located behind the Old Ship Church in Hingham.

George Boone, grandfather of Daniel, was born in 1666 in the village of Stoak in Devonshire, England. His Norman ancestors had left their homeland in 1066 at the time of William the Conqueror's conquest at the Battle of Hastings.

While a young man, George moved to Bradninch, England, where he married Mary Maugridge and found work as a weaver. He and his wife had seven sons and two daughters. He became a dissenter in 1707 at the age of forty-one and left the Church of England to become a member of the Religious Society of Friends. As a Quaker, he refused to take an oath of allegiance or to bear arms.

George had long dreamed of the day when he could move his family to America where William Penn had established his "Holy Experiment," a haven in Pennsylvania for all persecuted Christians, especially Quakers. He hoped his family could live there and worship according to their own religious convictions. Everyone was equal, regardless of religious or ethic background and there was justice and freedom for all.

George, a prudent man, did not want to endanger the lives of his entire family. So, before exposing his younger children to the dangers of the rough Atlantic and an unknown land, he sent ahead his three oldest children, George, Jr., Sarah and Squire. They were to report on the hazards of the ocean crossing, living conditions and availability of land on which to build a home.

2. Home of Samuel Lincoln (1619-1690) ancestor of President Lincoln. Samuel migrated from England to America in 1637 and built this house around 1650. Seven generations of Lincoln have occupied this residence in Hingham, Mass.

3. *Old Ship Church erected 1681, in Hingham, Massachusetts, and is the oldest continuously used structure for public worship in America. President Lincoln's ancestor, Samuel, occupied his private pew for worship. General Benjamin Lincoln,*

After a period of time and exchanges of correspondence, George decided conditions were favorable in the new land and lost little time moving his family from Bradninch, England to America. Anything that could not be carried on their backs was sold and the family walked seventy miles to the port of Bristol where he paid thirty-five pounds to board a small ship for the grueling ocean voyage.

During the eight-week crossing, the passengers were cooped up in the humid hold of the small, overcrowded vessel. Having to wear the same clothing throughout the crossing was most unpleasant, particularly for the women, but having to drink water which was barely potable and eat putrid salted meat was even more discouraging.

The stench of vomit caused by seasickness and the unsanitary necessity of collecting human excrement in buckets before tossing it overboard, was very offensive. Dysentery and scurvy took their toll. Those who died were buried at sea. Cold ocean water was all that was available for washing hands and faces. Despite the difficulties encountered, the Boone family was intact when the boat reached Philadelphia on October 10, 1717.

Chapter 2
Pennsylvania (1717)
Boone-Lincoln Families: Meeting,
Intermarriages and Migrations

In 1720, George Boone and most of his family settled along the Schuylkill River, where he bought four hundred acres nine miles downstream from present-day Reading in Oley (now Exeter Township), Berks County, Pennsylvania. The streams were full of fish and game was abundant in the woods. Daughter Sarah and her husband, Jacob Stover, had settled there earlier.

For a man of fifty-two with a family of nine, it was a tremendous undertaking to leave a home in England to start a new life in the American wilderness where marauding Indians were still a threat. One of their first new neighbors was Joseph Hanks (great-grandfather of Abraham Lincoln) and his family.

Since almost everything had to be made on the spot, basic tools were a necessity. The broadax was used to hew the logs for the outside walls of the cabin and to shape the beams for the interior. The dovetailed logs were chinked with clay to keep out the winter cold. A rough puncheon floor, hewn flat with an adz, was truly a luxury.

A small door was hung with leather hinges. The window, if there was one, probably was covered with paper and made rainproof by using lard or bear grease and would admit some light. The table, chairs and beds also were made by hand. A narrow wooden ladder led to a sleeping loft above.

The crudely built chimney made of logs and plastered with clay allowed most of the heat to escape in the winter. It was necessary to keep the fire going most of the time, because it was a chore to start a new one using flint and steel. If there was a sufficient supply of gunpowder, it could be ignited to start the fire. The pioneers burned pine knots at night to give a little light in their one-room cabins, although some made tallow candles which could be moved about the room.

In summer, cold spring water was used to keep meats, butter and cheese from spoiling. Meat was salted to preserve it in the winter.

When bedtime came, which was usually at sundown during cold weather, a warming pan filled with hot coals was placed under the covers to help take the chill from the beds.

The pioneer women, who labored from daybreak to sundown, were equal partners with the men in work and danger. They were toil-worn but invincible. The wife gave birth to a child about every two years, nursed it, prepared the family meals at the open fireplace, spun the thread, weaved the cloth and made the clothes.

She also milked the cow, gathered the eggs, churned the butter, made kettles of lye soap and frequently worked in the corn field alongside her husband. In addition to her many difficult household chores, she cared for the sick and acted as a midwife at births. At times, she was even called upon to protect her home and family from Indians.

Squire Boone had not joined the Boone family move to Oley. He remained several years in the village of North Wales, northeast of Philadelphia in Montgomery County, happy with the friendships he had made in the Welsh Quaker community. Here, according to the records of the Gwynedd Friends Monthly Meeting, Squire Boone and Sarah Morgan were married in the traditional form of Quaker meetings on September 23, 1720.

Squire had observed the decent interval of courtship prescribed by Quaker custom and a convocation certified his "Clearness from Other Women." The Friends of Meeting specifically prohibited cohabitation before marriage. Sarah produced a certificate of consent from her parents. The couple stood and said their vows and then signed a certificate along with their guests and 39 witnesses. In accordance with Friends tradition, there was no minister. John Hanks and Sarah Evans, relatives of Nancy Hanks, (President Lincoln's mother) also were married there shortly before moving to Berks County.

Mordecai Lincoln (son of Samuel) moved to Scituate, Massachusetts, where he built a home, gristmill and ironworks. He operated these until his death in 1727. He was buried in the Groveland Cemetery in North Scituate.

Mordecai Lincoln, Jr. previously had moved his family to Clarksburg in Freehold Township, Monmouth County, New Jersey. In 1727, he sold his deceased father's ironworks and gristmill in Scituate and bought a thousand acres in Amity, Exeter Township, Berks

4. *Girlhood home of Sarah Morgan, wife of Squire Boone - mother of Daniel, in North Wales, Montgomery County,*

5. *Gwynedd Friends Monthly Meeting House, located in North Wales, Montgomery County, Pennsylvania. Daniel Boone's father, Squire and mother Sarah Morgan, were married here in 1720.*

6. Home of Mordecai Lincoln, Sr. (son of Samuel and ancestor of President Abraham Lincoln) constructed in 1692, in

7. Grist Mill - constructed by Mordecai Lincoln, Sr., around 1691, in Scituate, Massachusetts.

8. Iron works factory constructed around 1710, by Mordecai Lincoln, Jr. (son of Mordecai, Sr.) in Clarksburg, Freehold

County and moved his family there where they became acquainted with the Boone clan.

On November 30, 1730, Squire Boone bought a tract of land along the Schuylkill River and built a log house, now known as the Daniel Boone Homestead, and moved his family to Exeter. His father and other relatives had settled there earlier.

While the Lincolns were attending their first Friends Monthly Meeting, they became acquainted with the Boone family. This was the beginning of a close relationship leading to several marriages between the two families that established strong ties that endured for many years.

Of necessity, families in those days were quite large. Squire and Sarah Boone's family was no exception. They had seven boys and four girls. Their sixth child, Daniel, was born November 2, 1734, in a log cabin surrounded by wilderness and hostile Indians. This was the beginning of a life story that was to quicken the pulse of the young and old alike for generations.

In 1736, the Exeter Friends Monthly Meeting was established and a log meeting house was erected on land donated by the elder George Boone. The charter members included four of the Boone family: George, Sr., George, Jr., Sarah and Squire.

A short time later, the elder Mordecai Lincoln died and was buried in the cemetery that George Boone, Sr., had given to the Exeter Meeting. Daniel became a close boyhood friend of Abraham Lincoln, grandson of Mordecai, Jr. and the great-great grandfather of our sixteenth president. This friendship strengthened ties between the families.

The families were well-acquainted by the time the first of many intermarriages took place. William Boone, son of George, Jr., married Sarah Lincoln, daughter of Mordecai, Jr., in 1738.

According to custom, a Quaker youth was to inform the girl's parents of his intentions before he came to court or became emotionally involved in any way with their daughter. He was to receive permission from the girl's father before taking his daughter's hand in marriage. Nevertheless, the girl was not forced into marriage against her will. If she knew she was pregnant at the time of the wedding, she was required to make a public acknowledgment.

9. *Former home of Mordecai Lincoln, Jr. (great-great-grandfather of President Abraham Lincoln) built about 1733, in Amity, Exeter Township, Berks County, Pennsylvania. It is now*

10. *Mordecai Lincoln's home, restored in 1992. Berks County, Pennsylvania. Exeter Township, Amity.*

11. *Daniel Boone Homestead, in Oley, Exeter Township, Berks County, Pennsylvania. This stone building covers the site of the log cabin where Daniel was born in 1734.*

After the simple ceremony, guests were invited to the bride's home where a feast, including tea and wine, was served. All male guests were to receive a kiss from the bride. Any form of music, singing, dancing or card-playing was forbidden. The newlyweds stayed with the bride's parents for about two weeks before moving to their own house.

The patriarch, George Boone, was seventy-eight when he died February 2, 1744 and he was buried in the Exeter Friends of Meeting Cemetery. In keeping with Quaker custom, there was no gravestone.

The cemetery was unlike most others. When it was filled to capacity, Meeting members hauled in additional dirt to cover the original graves to a depth of four feet. Then they started a second tier of plots atop the first level. Today, about half of the second level is filled and only members of Friends of Meeting may be buried there. Descendants of the Boone and Lincoln families were buried in the Exeter Friends of Meeting Cemetery as recently as 1895.

The Boones and the Lincolns accepted their responsibilities in community and state affairs. George Boone, Jr. was a justice of the peace and a surveyor. Thomas Lincoln became township sheriff. Squire Boone worked as a blacksmith, gunsmith and weaver. Daniel's Uncle John was a school teacher.

Abraham Lincoln, the great-great-uncle of the sixteenth president, became county commissioner, assemblyman and, in 1789-90, was a delegate to the Pennsylvania Convention for ratifying the United States Constitution. He was selected to make the address to General Washington at Philadelphia. In 1760, he married Daniel's cousin, Ann, daughter of James Boone.

It was evident at an early age that Daniel had qualities that would make him different. He did not attend school while growing up but spent most of his time in the wilderness. What little he did learn about reading and writing was taught by his sister-in-law, Sarah, the wife of his older brother, Samuel.

For six summers, Daniel and his mother took their herd of cattle about four miles into the high mountain pasture. They seldom returned home during this time and Daniel grew closer to his mother than any of her other children. It was his mother's influence that instilled in him a lifelong belief in the Quaker faith. Daniel's job was to

12. *Exeter Friends Meeting House and Burying Ground. First a log house, established in 1725, replaced by stone in 1759, located in Exeter Township, Berks County, Pennsylvania. Daniel Boone's grandfather donated the land for the house and cemetery. George Boone, Sr. and Mordecai Lincoln, Jr. were buried here. There are no grave markers. The cemetery contains two layers of graves.*

protect the cows from wolves and Indians and to help his mother with the milking, making cheese and churning butter.

Daniel found time between chores to build himself a bark shelter in the forest, still deeper into Indian territory. There he learned most of his wilderness skills and strengthened his courage and independence.

Once Daniel was absent from camp for several days. A search party was guided to Daniel's newly constructed shelter by a distant curl of smoke rising into the clear summer sky. He was found sitting inside on a bearskin, roasting a piece of fresh meat over an open fire. The rest of the neatly skinned bear hung nearby.

"Are you lost?" they asked.

"No," he said, as he handed each a piece of freshly roasted bear meat. That marked the beginning of Daniel's solitary life-style in the woods.

In his early teens, Daniel learned many things that prepared him for his adventurous life. He searched out the course of the streams, tested the quality of the land, learned the location of salt licks and followed the trails of Indians and wild game. He also mastered basic farming and cattle-raising techniques and the art of blacksmithing, including forging, welding and mending guns and wagons.

Daniel was fascinated by the Indians. He became their loyal friend and came to understand their motives, cunningness, strategies, tricks, traits and habits. As they shared their secrets, Daniel learned to start fires without flint and steel, to select the best firewood for cooking, the right bark for making a night's shelter and to gather the softest evergreen boughs for bedding.

He became adept at moving silently through the woods and hiding, when necessary, to study the creatures of the forest. His skills enabled him to observe the habits of fur-bearing animals, such as beaver, muskrat and otter. He was to earn a lifelong living from their pelts.

When Daniel was twelve, his father gave him his first rifle. He took to it at once and soon became an expert rifleman and the main provider of wild game for the family table.

Even though the Boone family had donated the land for the Friends of Meeting house and cemetery, they had difficulty being accepted by the members. When Daniel's sister, Sarah, married John Wilcoxen she was promptly censured for "marrying out" as were her parents for allowing it to happen. The three expressed contrition in public.

Seven months later, a committee of Quaker ladies found that Sarah had been pregnant before she was married and this was sufficient reason to expel her from the Meeting. Israel, Daniel's older brother, also married out and was disowned by the Exeter Meeting, but his father, Squire, who occasionally indulged in strong drink, refused to humble himself again.

Ironically, Squire's father had dissented from the Church of England, just a half century earlier and now, he braced himself to reject the dissenters. The records of the monthly Meeting in Exeter, relating to the Boone family, ended in 1748.

Daniel retained his Quaker beliefs throughout his life. He never hated the Indians, although they were a constant threat to life for most people along the frontier.

Several things of a critical nature happened within a few short years to induce the Boones, along with other friends and relatives, to consider leaving Berks County. First, the Boones desired to escape the embarrassing censure imposed upon their family by the Meeting. On top of that, the soil was being depleted and game was growing scarce. Finally, and most important, the Boones preferred to live on the fringe of civilization, not in the middle of it.

Chapter 3
Virginia (1750)
Boones-Lincolns Settle in
Buckingham County

In 1750, Squire Boone sold his farm to a relative, William Maugridge. Squire then started what could be called the Boone-Lincoln migration when he, with his brothers John and George, and John Lincoln (son of Mordecai, Jr.), moved to Virginia near Winchester. Joseph Hanks (grandfather of Nancy) and Joseph Bryan (father of Rebecca, who later became Daniel's wife) left Pennsylvania at the same time.

John Lincoln, better known as "Virginia John" (Abe's great grandfather), later settled near Linville Creek in Rockingham County where he spent the remainder of his life. He and his wife, Rebecca, were buried in a small family cemetery on the side of the hill above the creek. A short distance from the grave site is a house built in 1800 by Jacob Lincoln (third son of Virginia John). The house still stands and has been occupied continuously.

Daniel was fifteen when his family began its southward journey through the Cumberland Valley of Maryland and crossed the Potomac River at Harpers Ferry.

En route, they lingered for awhile in Winchester, Virginia, staying with friends who had previously left Exeter and had settled in the Shenandoah Valley of Virginia. (The valley is a natural passageway between the Allegheny and the Blue Ridge Mountains.)

Their longest stay was at Linville Creek in Rockingham County. Daniel's Aunt Sarah, her husband, Jacob Stover, and family had preceded them to the area. Thomas Lincoln (Abe's father) was born there in 1778. It was there, too, that Virginia John's younger sister, Ann, and her husband, William Tallman, were living when their son, Benjamin, married Dinnah Boone, a daughter of Benjamin Boone. Squire set up a blacksmith shop and did some scratch farming.

In this migration, Joseph Hanks and his family settled on the outskirts of Alexandria between the Potomac and Rappahannock rivers,

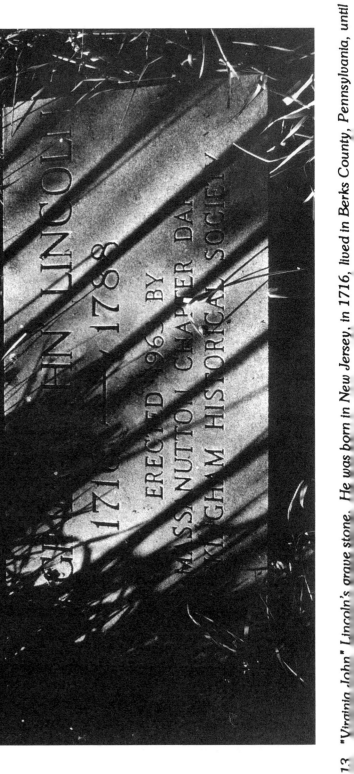

13. "Virginia John" Lincoln's grave stone. He was born in New Jersey, in 1716, lived in Berks County, Pennsylvania, until

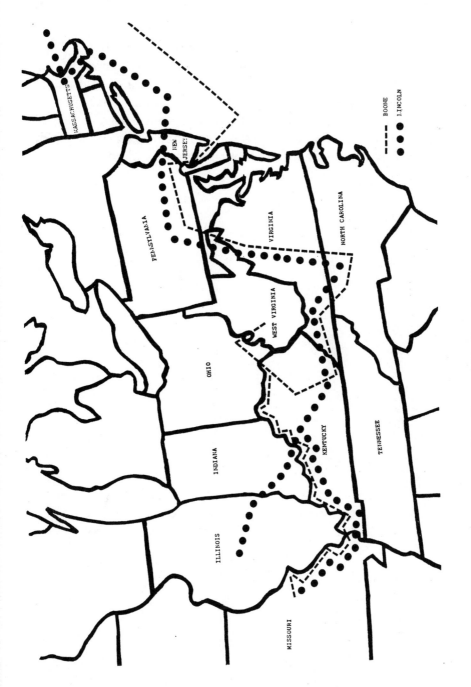

14. *Boone-Lincoln migrations*

where they farmed for a livelihood. Joseph Bryan's family settled in the Yadkin River Valley of North Carolina.

During the ensuing year, 1751, Daniel and his friend, Henry Miller, ventured about two hundred miles south, stalking game in the headwaters of the Yadkin. They found an abundance of wild game, plenty of fruits and nuts and fertile land for cultivation. Their greatest find was an area which was mostly rugged wilderness. After a year of hunting and trapping, Daniel and Henry returned home loaded with pelts which they sold in Philadelphia for thirteen hundred dollars.

Chapter 4
North Carolina (1752)
Boones on The Yadkin

Daniel was so enthusiastic about his discoveries in the Yadkin Valley that he persuaded his father to move there the following year. The family spent the first winter in a cave on the east bank of the Yadkin at a point now known as Boones Ford.

During that winter, Daniel and his father trapped and hunted full time. They accumulated a large quantity of pelts which they sold in the spring of 1753.

With the proceeds, they bought their first 640 acres, on which they built a log cabin. This parcel was located a few miles northeast of Mocksville along Dutchman Creek. A short time later, they purchased another 640 acres along Bear Creek.

It was in the wilderness area that Daniel honed his hunting and woodcraft skills to a fine point. His expertise in handling the rifle was unsurpassed by any other frontiersman. Once, when he was passing through the small frontier village of Salisbury, his horse laden with a fresh catch of furs, two strangers challenged him to a shooting match with a small wager to make it interesting.

The three proceeded to a nearby field, where Daniel soon relieved them of ten dollars. One of the strangers then said, "I'll bet one hundred dollars against your furs on one more shot."

It was the old story of taking advantage of the "dumb hick from the sticks." A pre-cut target was in the trunk of a nearby tree and Daniel needed only a quick glance to see that there was already a bullet hole on the rim of the bull's-eye.

His opponent's rifle pulled slightly to the side as he fired and he missed the tree entirely. Daniel congratulated him on a fine shot but was not fooled by the hoax. He then put his bullet squarely through the center of the bull's-eye, ending the contest. Daniel went home with $110 and his pelts and was never challenged again by those two "slickers."

15. *Boone Cave, on the east bank of the Yadkin River, near Mocksville, North Carolina, at a point now known as Boones*

16. *Replica of Squire Boone's first cabin built in North Carolina located in the Daniel Boone State Park above the Yadkin River southeast of Mocksville.*

Chapter 5
The War Years (1754-1814)
French and Indian War, Cherokee War
Lord Dunmore's War,
American Revolutionary War, and
War of 1812

During Daniel's late teens, the French and British struggled for supremacy in the New World to determine control of the North American continent.

The French navigated the waterways of the St. Lawrence River, crossed the Great Lakes and traveled down the Ohio and Mississippi rivers to New Orleans. They occasionally built forts along the waterways, giving them an inland communication advantage.

Meanwhile, the British colonists were inching their way cautiously from the tidelands through the Piedmont area across the rugged Appalachian Mountain barrier on their westward move into Indian territory, searching for fertile new land and a fresh supply of game. They cut trees, built homes and killed game. This steady encroachment enraged the Indians, who were ready for the warpath.

Since the French fur traders refrained from settling in Indian territory, a mutual trust and friendly relationship developed between them. The British, on the other hand, became the natural enemy of the French and the Indians.

France was the greatest military power in Europe at that time but had only isolated forts scattered over a wide territory in North America. The French outnumbered the British in Europe five to two, but the British outnumbered the French in North America fourteen to one.

The French were willing to supply the Indians with guns and ammunition and were more than anxious to have them as allies. This was the beginning of the French and Indian War (1754-63) also known in Europe as the Seven Years War.

The immediate struggle was for control of the Ohio River Valley. The French had constructed Fort Duquesne (now Pittsburgh) and the British sent General Edward Braddock to dislodge them. This action proved to be a catastrophe for the British forces.

In February 1755, Daniel, now twenty-one, enlisted in Captain Edward B. Dobbs's regiment of the North Carolina Militia. Then he went north to serve as a blacksmith and supply wagoner under General Braddock in the battle at Fort Duquesne.

During this engagement, Daniel met Lieutenant Colonel George Washington, who was twenty-three. Washington had strongly urged Braddock to deploy his soldiers rather than use the European close-rank or frontal formation, but to no avail. He spoke from experience, because he had been defeated and captured two years earlier at Fort Necessity while employing the same formation Braddock was now using.

Braddock boasted that he would capture the fort within three or four days, but he had doomed his soldiers and himself from the start. He was killed, along with three-fourths of his men, and was buried in the middle of the road so Indians could not find his body.

Washington narrowly escaped with his life, although he did have four bullet holes in his coat. He managed to restore order out of a catastrophic situation by leading a retreat that saved the lives of Braddock's remaining soldiers.

Daniel and John Finley, a fellow wagoner, were seized with panic and fled for their lives by cutting the traces from their team of horses and riding away. It was said that this was the only battle in which Daniel fought that he did not emerge as a hero.

Daniel's close association with Finley during the battle at Fort Duquesne turned out to be another decisive influence in his life. Finley was one of the few white men who had found his way into the unexplored wilderness of Kentucky. Wild game was plentiful there, including great herds of deer and buffalo. He had spent several months in the Kentucky wilds trading furs with the Shawnee Indians. At one time, they had held him captive but later released him.

Daniel spent many hours around the campfires listening to Finley's vivid tales about his Kentucky adventures. The stories fired Daniel's imagination and became an irresistible force pushing him to explore the Kentucky wilderness at the first possible opportunity.

After General Braddock's defeat at Fort Duquesne, Daniel returned home to Yadkin Valley where he resumed his hunting and trapping. One day, however, his trapping did an about-face. He momentarily caught "buck fever" and was entangled in a "female snare" set by an attractive sixteen-year-old, Miss Rebecca Bryan (daughter of Joseph Bryan). She had diverted his attention just long enough to spring the trap.

Although Daniel was nearly twenty-two at the time, he was still very shy around girls. Even so, he did not hesitate to pursue the girl he really wanted. On August 14, 1756, after a frontier courtship of about a year, Daniel and Rebecca were married by his father, who was a justice of the peace in Rowan County. A preacher was not available because no church had been established on the frontier.

Family, friends and neighbors gathered for a feast of fresh venison and cornbread, while a jug of moonshine whiskey was passed around freely. It was late when the groom and blushing bride climbed the narrow ladder to the sleeping loft above, amid an abundance of suggestive jokes and advice. The giggling of the young girls subsided as everyone except the immediate family went home.

Then Daniel turned to Becky and they started a marriage which lasted fifty-six years. It was mostly a happy union but not without considerable grief. Their marriage was the second union between the two families, since Daniel's younger sister, Mary, had married William Bryan (Rebecca's brother) in 1754.

At that early time, Becky's father, Joseph, and grandfather, Morgan Bryan, who were Quakers, also migrated from Pennsylvania and were the most prominent settlers in the Yadkin Valley. However, it was not until the Boones and the Bryans reached the valley that a close relationship was established. It continued for many generations during which several intermarriages took place. Over the next twenty-five years, Becky gave birth to six boys and four girls during a time of few comforts and little peace.

Soon after their marriage, in 1757, Daniel built a cabin on Sugar Tree Creek, a tributary of Dutchman's Creek, two miles east of the present town of Farmington, North Carolina. Later, when he found the smoke from his cabin was no longer the only smoke that floated into the air along the Yadkin, he realized it was getting too crowded for him and built a cabin on Bear Creek.

Three years later, Daniel enlisted in the militia under Colonel Forbes and went north once again to help Colonel Washington oust the French and Indians from Fort Duquesne. That time, not a shot was fired because the enemy had burned the fort and withdrawn.

The French and Indian War was the last conflict in which the colonists carried the British flag into battle or defended the crown with their bravery. The high cost of that war may have been one of the primary reasons the British began to impose taxes on the colonists.

Spain had allied with the French during the war. When the war was over, Spain had lost Florida and England had acquired Canada and all the territory east of the Mississippi River, except New Orleans. To compensate for the loss of Florida, France gave Spain New Orleans and the Louisiana Territory west of the Mississippi.

France finally lost all control of its North American holdings during September 1759 in the decisive battles on the Plains of Abraham at Quebec. The superior British Navy was a critical factor in the final outcome. That victory may have been the beginning of the colonists' separation from the British. About this time, they began to call themselves Americans.

Daniel once again volunteered for the militia during the frontier war with the Cherokees. He moved his family to Culpeper County, Virginia, where they escaped the fury of the Indians during the war. He was very valuable when it came to spying on the Indians, because he knew them better than any white man on the frontier. He understood their way of thinking, how they would act under adverse conditions, their weaknesses, their strategy and their bravery.

As the war drew to a close, Daniel returned home with his family to continue his farming, blacksmithing and weaving. He was not too fond of farming and in 1760, he turned to hunting and trapping full time. He asked his younger brother, Edward, (Ned) who was single, to look after his family and left the farming to Becky and the children, but he was careful not to plant more than they could tend.

Daniel's first solitary trip of any duration was into the Tennessee wilderness. There he carved on a tree, "D. Boone cilled A. Bar."

He found that roof, house and bed were not absolute necessities and clothing was seldom changed. Later, he would be away from home as long as two years at a time, leaving Becky to wonder whether he was dead or alive.

On Daniel's return home in 1762 from a twenty-month trip, Becky presented him with a new baby girl, much to his surprise. It seems that Ned had comforted Becky in her bereavement over the apparent loss of her husband and she became pregnant. Since Daniel had been captured by the Indians, they thought he was dead.

Daniel could understand that and, realizing the last name was the same, he accepted and loved baby Jemima as his own daughter without ever mentioning the situation again. He lived out his last days in Jemima's home in Missouri and he and Ned remained very close for many years until Ned was killed by Indians.

Another wedding took place between the two families when Benjamin Lincoln (born in 1745 and the grandson of Mordecai, Jr.) married Dinah Boone (daughter of Benjamin Boone, a cousin of Daniel's).

At times, Daniel would return home loaded with furs and sometimes without a single pelt. Hostile Indians would relieve him of his catch, causing him to go into debt for supplies needed for his next hunting trip. Daniel's indebtedness was to follow him most of his life.

By 1764, the frontier was overtaken by civilization. A lesser breed of men was moving into the area and killing more game than necessary. Daniel bought 640 acres in the Brushy Mountains along Beaver Creek, now Ferguson, on the upper Yadkin, eight miles west of Wilkesboro. That was to be his last home before leaving North Carolina.

During his formative years, Daniel's young son, James, spent much of his time in the woods hunting with his father. They sat around the campfire at night, before bedding down under the stars, giving Daniel time to reminisce about his friend, John Finley, and his exciting stories about Kentucky.

Upon returning home in January 1765 from a hunting trip, Daniel learned of his father's death. He was grief-stricken. Squire was buried in Joppa Cemetery in Mocksville.

Daniel had heard about Dr. Thomas Walker's surveying trip in 1750 during which he discovered an Indian warrior's path through the Cumberland Gap, the gateway to eastern Kentucky. Dr. Walker built the first cabin in Kentucky near there. Christopher Geist, the first known white man to see the Kentucky River, was lead scout for the expedition.

Dr. Walker was a delegate to the Revolutionary Convention in Philadelphia, a physician, a surveyor, and guardian of Thomas

17. Bricks encasing the tombstones of Squire Boone and Sarah Morgan Boone (parents of Daniel) in the Joppa Cemetery in Mocksville, North Carolina.

18. Cumberland Gap, gateway to eastern Kentucky. The first white man to see the gap was Christopher Geist who later became the lead guide and scout for Dr. Thomas Walker's surveying trip in 1750. Daniel Boone built the Wilderness Trail

Jefferson after Jefferson's father died. In 1741, Dr. Walker married Mildred Meriwether, a second cousin of George Washington.

Daniel had searched many times for the gap but without success. It was in the spring of 1767 that Daniel and his younger brother, Squire, and William Hall tried to locate the passageway. They entered Kentucky near the Breaks of Virginia at the headwaters of the Levisa Fork in the Big Sandy River Valley. They were unsuccessful because they were too far northeast. They were literally lost in the valley near present Louisa and Prestonsburg for a cold, miserable winter. The following spring, in frustration, they returned home in disgust.

To Daniel's great pleasure, waiting for him, besides his own family, was John Finley, who thirteen years earlier had promised him a guided trip through the gap to Kentucky. The two spent the entire winter of 1768 making preparations for Daniel's first journey through the Cumberland Gap. If Finley had not shown up at that time, it is doubtful Daniel would have played such an important part in the early history of Kentucky.

Daniel had evolved into a new type of frontiersman. He was sun-browned and wore a beaver cap, leather moccasins, deerskin jacket and trousers and had a flintlock rifle in hand. A tomahawk, hunting knife, bullet pouch and powder horn hung from his belt. His looks and actions were more those of an Indian than a white man.

It was a warm, sunny day on May 1, 1769, when Daniel reluctantly gave up his tranquil domestic happiness for awhile. He bade his understanding wife and children good-bye. He, Finley and four companions--John Stewart (Daniel's brother-in-law), Jim Mooney, Joe Holden and Bill Cooley--all experienced hunters, left the Yadkin Valley in search of the elusive Cumberland Gap.

By that time, Daniel had lost all interest in farming, so it was agreed that his brother, Squire, would remain behind to look after their families until the corn crops were harvested in the fall. His son, James, now eleven, would keep meat on the family table.

Daniel was now heavily in debt for horses, food and supplies and at that very moment was under summons to appear at the March term of court in Salisbury for nonpayment of his debts. Later, when the summons was posted at the courthouse, someone wrote across the front of it, "G o n T o K a n t u k."

For the first few days, the group traveled through territory known well to Daniel and Stewart. But after leaving Martin's Station, the white man's last outpost, a new sight was around every turn. The greatest thrill for Daniel was the first sight of the Cumberland Gap which had eluded him so long.

As they penetrated farther into the wilderness, they became aware of a new danger. They were now following what seemed to be a trail used by generations of warring Indian tribes, the Cherokee from the south and the Shawnee of the north. However, since the Indians did not make a permanent home in the Kentucky wilderness, but came only to hunt or to make war on each other, it was unlikely the group would run into any.

They were about four hundred miles from home on June 7 when they set up their first base camp in the Red River Valley on a fork of the Kentucky River. They called it Station Camp Creek. A half-faced camp was built of logs, with a fireplace on the open side and boughs overhead.

For the next several months, their time was spent hunting by day and skinning their kill at night. It was not long before they had accumulated a large cache of skins from buffalo, deer, elk, bear, beaver and otter.

One day, when Daniel and Stewart were hunting together, as they usually did, they were trapped in a meadow by a large herd of stampeding buffalo. Stewart started to run, but Daniel grabbed him just in time and pulled him to the ground.

Daniel knew it would be impossible to outrun a charging herd of buffalo. He also knew he would have only one shot to try to save their lives. He waited with steel-like nerves until the lead bull was only twenty feet away. Taking careful aim, he pulled the trigger of his trusty rifle, "Ticklicker." A moment later, the bull's legs buckled and it tumbled to the ground, landing directly in front of them. They immediately took cover behind the large mountain of fur as the stampeding buffalo rushed past on either side.

Daniel was now beginning to take stock of himself and their surroundings. It was a daily occurrence to encounter deer, elk and buffalo herds, wild turkey flocks and other forest creatures. They had observed with awe the many wildflowers, sparkling clear streams and fertile soil, along with large, sturdy hardwood trees filled with songbirds acting as ready sentinels of the forest.

In reality, though, there was a risk of life and liberty where cunning was the law of the wilderness. Sooner or later, they would have to reckon with the power of the Indians. By now the news surely had spread throughout the Indian nations about the paleface who had come to slaughter their game.

One day, as Daniel was hunting alone, he encountered an elderly Indian who had been left to die beside the trail. Daniel made him comfortable and, before leaving him, went into the forest to retrieve some deer meat for the old warrior.

At heart, Daniel was very gentle and kind. He had the courage and boldness of a lion but would avoid danger as long as he could. However, when no other course was open, he would stand up and fight as long as necessary.

Daniel and his companions fared well through the summer and fall. The prolonged absence of a foe may have lulled them into a sense of false security. That was soon to change.

Just before Christmas, Daniel and Stewart were caught off guard by an armed band of Shawnees. Daniel immediately extended his hand in friendship but, at the same time, was reluctant to disclose the location of their cache of skins. He also knew if he did not reveal the whereabouts of the furs, he and Stewart would be killed.

The Indians took everything--pelts, guns and horses. The Indians then started north with their captives, probably with the intent of adopting them into their tribe.

As captives, Daniel and Stewart realized that everything they had worked for during the past several months was gone. Daniel knew the Indians' thinking extremely well, so he presumed that by exercising patience and confidence they would be able to escape.

His plan was to pretend that he liked them and to show no fear or any desire to escape, which was difficult for Stewart to do. After seven days on the trail, they apparently had won the confidence of their captors, because that night all of the Indians were sound asleep at the same time. Daniel, rising cautiously from his feigned sleep, gently awakened the slumbering Stewart. They retrieved a gun and a powderhorn, then disappeared into the darkness. Once out of sight, each second was precious to gain time and distance as they traveled quickly through the dense forest.

When the Indians awoke the next morning and found the pair missing, they apparently decided it was too late for pursuit. When Daniel and Stewart arrived back at the base camp, they found it had been plundered by Indians and abandoned by Finley and his three companions. Daniel did not see or hear of Finley again. He grieved over the loss of a friendship which started with their escape during Braddock's defeat at Fort Duquesne back in 1755. Much credit should be given to Finley, for he alone was responsible for Daniel's great interest in the Kentucky wilderness.

Daniel and Stewart found it difficult to carry on hunting and trapping activities with only one horse, one rifle and a small amount of ammunition. They supplemented their meager food supply with fresh meat, fruits, nuts and berries. They now realized that their previous efforts in learning the ways of the forest were not in vain.

Everything seemed to be going fairly well when, one day after a hunt, Stewart failed to show up at the designated rendezvous. His remains were found two years later in a tree hollow. He apparently had been shot and scalped. Of the six original hunters who left home more than two years earlier, Daniel was now the only one remaining. The reason for Daniel's survival was his knowledge of the Indians and his alertness. For instance, he could dodge a bullet from a rifle after seeing the smoke when the gun was fired.

Not knowing if any of them were still alive, Squire and Alex Neeley, after the fall crops had been harvested, set out in search of Daniel's base camp, which was more than four hundred miles into the wilderness. They located it a month later and Daniel jumped with joy to see his brother and to learn of the welfare of his family and the love they had sent to him. He also was pleased to see the horses and supplies they had brought.

The horses were invaluable but a source of great anxiety, because they were just what would be most likely to betray them to the Indians. They could not be hidden as the men could hide and would let their presence be known by a whinny if any Indians were nearby.

After a day or so of celebration, the three set about hunting again. Neeley was wounded during a skirmish with the Indians and died a few days later, leaving Daniel and Squire alone in hostile territory. Stewart and Neeley were the first two white men known to have died in the battle for Kentucky.

The brothers continued hunting until they had a sufficient supply of pelts. Then they decided that Squire would return home with their cache, sell the furs, pay off some of their debts, secure fresh supplies and ammunition and return to do more hunting. It took great courage for the brothers to say good-bye in the wilderness, because each knew of the dangers the other faced.

There must have been great love and confidence between them to part in that way. If Squire had failed in his return trip home, Daniel might have been lost to history. Daniel was alone again in the wilderness, without bread, salt, sugar or even the company of a horse or dog. That, indeed, was complete solitude.

During the three months Squire was away, Daniel did a considerable amount of exploring. He traveled as far as the falls on the Ohio River. At night he slept in a canebrake, fearful of being caught alone by the Indians. One day, while reclining in the forest and listening to the chatter of the tree dwellers and thinking of Becky and the children, he found himself surrounded by Indians. The chief was brandishing a knife. Daniel smiled calmly as he extended his hand in a gesture of friendship and the chief, unexpectedly, handed him the knife. Daniel suddenly opened his mouth, pretending to swallow the knife, but let it slip into his open shirt. He then retrieved the knife, calmly handing it back to the chief. Thinking the knife was bewitched, the chief threw it into the forest and the Indians disappeared.

Before Squire had left for home, a date had been set for his return. On July 27, 1771, both arrived at the base camp. Squire brought the news from home and fresh supplies and equipment.

The brothers continued their hunting through the fall and winter and had accumulated all the furs the horses would be able to pack out. At that point, Daniel said, "Let's take our cache of furs home, pay off our debts, then return to Kentucky with our families and make this our permanent home."

Several days later, as they approached the gap on their way home, a band of Cherokees met them on the trail and took their horses, furs and supplies. Daniel hated to go home without anything to show for two years of hard work and, even worse, poorer than the day he left home. Squire thought they should be thankful to be alive.

Becky and the children were overwhelmed with joy to see Daniel when he arrived home and they and the neighbors listened intently to the exciting stories he told.

Daniel created a lot of excitement throughout the Yadkin Valley in 1772 about his proposed family move into the Kentucky wilderness. Becky realized how much Daniel wanted to move there, but it was still no easy task for him to persuade her to go where no other white woman had been before, especially when six experienced hunters, including Stewart and Finley, had lost their lives there within the past three years.

As the winter months faded into spring, it became evident that Daniel's labors were not in vain, because by then five other families had expressed a desire to join in the wilderness adventure. It was proof that Daniel's calm recital was having its effect throughout the valley. It was early summer when a final decision was made by the six families to take the risk. James Boone, now seventeen, could hardly wait to get started.

Now that the decision had been made, preparations for the long, treacherous journey through the rugged mountainous country was an around-the-clock job. A tentative date of September 25, 1773, had been set and Daniel sold the farm and all of their household goods.

When the day of departure arrived, the cows, chickens and dogs were ready for travel and the horses were loaded with the family's necessities. Becky and the younger children climbed aboard. The family's clothing was placed in a deerskin bag which hung from the saddlehorn of Becky's horse.

Daniel, Becky and their eight children were joined by five other families as they left the valley. Daniel, now thirty-eight, was leading his first family group through the Cumberland Gap to the wilderness of Kentucky. For the first half day of travel, they were accompanied by a group of neighbors and relatives, including Daniel's mother, Sarah, seventy-three. When it was time to say good-bye, she and Daniel wept freely as they embraced each other.

At first, travel was northwest through the present town of Boone, then into Tennessee and Virginia where the group was joined by others from the Clinch River Valley. Turning westward through Powell Valley, they met a small group of Becky's relatives. In addition,

Michael Stoner and Captain William Russell, with forty armed men, joined the pioneers.

Squire was familiar with the trails, because he had traveled them several times before. He knew the overnight camping spots that would offer shelter and a fresh water supply. At twilight on October 9, the fifteenth day on the trail, they decided to make three separate campsites for the night at Wallen's Ridge.

Daniel was up front with several riflemen. His son, James, and Captain Russell's son, Henry, along with six other companions--James and Richard Mendenhall, Isaac Crabtree, a man named Drake and two slaves, Adam and Charles--were about two miles back, tending the cattle. Bringing up the rear another mile or so back were the families and the other riflemen.

That night, James Boone and his companions sat around the campfire, discussing their adventures and listening to the screech owls and nighthawks. Later on, they bedded down for the night, feeling good about their progress so far.

At daybreak, they were ambushed by a group of Shawnee Indians. Henry and James were shot in the hip and tortured by having their fingernails pulled out. Their hands were slashed to shreds while they were trying to protect themselves. They pleaded for their lives but to no avail. When they finally realized it was hopeless, James pleaded for the Indians to end his life quickly.

Although wounded, Isaac and a slave, Adam, managed to crawl to cover in the underbrush. Charlie, the other slave, was taken prisoner and an argument ensued among the Indians, prompting one of them to split open Charlie's head with a tomahawk.

Daniel was awakened by the rifle shots, but it was too late by the time he reached the site of the massacre. Adam emerged from his hiding place and told Daniel the gruesome story of how horribly the boys had suffered before dying.

Losing their oldest son was a tremendous blow to the Boone family. They buried him beside the trail, wrapped in a white linen sheet his mother had brought from home. His father put heavy rocks on the grave to prevent the wolves from digging it up. During the next several years, Daniel often visited the grave site to make sure it had not been disturbed.

Daniel and Squire still wanted to go to Kentucky where Daniel dreamed of his family spending their first winter together in the wilderness, but the others wanted to return to the Yadkin Valley. Since the two Boone families had sold their farms in North Carolina, they decided to relocate in the Clinch River Valley near Castlewood, Virginia, until they could resume their journey into Kentucky.

The women and children spent two miserable winters there in a log cabin that had been abandoned. Little farming was done, because they had not intended to make it a permanent home. They subsisted mostly on venison and bear meat. By that time, Daniel had little money left from the sale of his farm. He was in great despair for a time over the loss of his son and his thwarted plans for settling in Kentucky.

When news about the vicious attack by the Indians spread through the frontier in 1774, it caused frequent conflicts to break out on either side of the mountain barrier. These skirmishes became known as Lord Dunmore's War. During that time, Daniel was requested by Lord Dunmore, the royal governor of Virginia, to make a quick trip to the falls on the Ohio River, near present Louisville, to warn a group of surveyors of an impending Indian attack.

Daniel, accompanied by Michael Stoner, an experienced pioneer, immediately started on the journey. After they had traveled about five hundred miles, they met Captain James Harrod and forty-one men who were building several cabins near present Harrodsburg. Harrod and his men had navigated down the Ohio River to the area. Daniel would have liked to build a cabin for his family, but the Indians had different ideas. The red man would not stand by and let the white man encroach upon his hunting grounds without putting up a fearful resistance.

While Harrod and his men were building their cabins, the second to be built in Kentucky, they were fired upon by the Shawnees and two white men were killed. The others decided to join Daniel and Stoner in their trip to the falls.

They traveled sixty-two days through Indian territory to reach their destination, which was about eight hundred miles from the Clinch Valley. Harrod and his men returned later to build the first permanent settlement in Kentucky, now known as Harrodsburg.

For the next few days, several skirmishes with the Indians took place along the Ohio River as the party proceeded in a northeasterly

19. *Artist's conception of Daniel Boone at approximate age 40*

20. Interior of restored Fort Harrod. In 1774, Captain James Harrod and his men came down the Ohio River to build the

direction, eventually arriving at the confluence of the Kanawha River. The site is now known as the Battle of Point Pleasant in West Virginia.

Even though most credit was given to the minutemen at Lexington, some historians contend the first American Revolution battle was fought at Point Pleasant. General Andrew Lewis and Daniel, soon to be Captain Boone, were selected by Governor Dunmore to lead eleven hundred colonial forces, the Virginia Raiders, against the Shawnees led by Chief Cornstalk. The Indians were allied with the redcoats. British Governor Henry Hamilton, commander at Fort Detroit, was supplying guns and ammunition to them while paying a price for each white man's scalp. Daniel's main responsibility was to spy on the Indians for General Lewis.

In the fiercest Indian battle ever to be fought east of the Mississippi, seventy-five colonists were killed and 140 wounded. The battle ended on October 10, 1774, when Chief Cornstalk found he was on the losing side of the engagement and was forced to retreat across the Ohio.

There he called a war council and asked, "Shall we kill our women and children and then go and fight until we all die?" Silence ensued.

Chief Cornstalk then said, "I'll go ask for peace."

Three years later, Daniel heard that Chief Cornstalk and his son had been shot down by colonial soldiers at Fort Randolph, though they had come under a flag of truce. The great chief had tried desperately to be a friend to the white man, but it cost him his life. This action would further inflame his people to make war against the white man.

Although the Indians chose not to live in Kentucky, neither did they want the white man to settle there, cut their trees and kill their game. The treaty that Daniel made with Chief Cornstalk at Point Pleasant gave the Virginians the right to settle in Kentucky, but the Cherokee tribe of the south did not recognize the treaty. The Cherokees also claimed the same hunting grounds as the Shawnees and demanded payment from the pioneers for their share of the land.

When Daniel returned home, a true pioneer, he was given a military commission, his first, as a captain by the State of Virginia in recognition of his abilities as a peacemaker and negotiator with the Indians. He was one white man the Indians trusted.

Captain Boone's family and neighbors throughout Clinch Valley were proud of him because he was chosen for such an arduous task

21. *The fiercest Indian battle ever fought east of the Mississippi and, the first battle of the American Revolution, when General Andrew Lewis and Captain Daniel Boone led the Virginia Raiders against the Shawnee under Chief Cornstalk who was allied with the British. Governor Henry Hamilton, commander at Fort Detroit, supplied the Shawnee with guns and ammunition and paid them for white mans scalp. Located in Point*

and had the confidence of the head of state. This type of recognition was to continue most of his life. Boone's selection by the governor made him feel that his previous risks with the Indians and the hardships he had endured in the wilderness were not all in vain.

Boone became acquainted with Colonel Richard Henderson from Virginia, who had settled recently in North Carolina where he became interested in politics and was later appointed to a judgeship. Boone was behind constantly in payments on his debts for the shot and powder needed for his hunting expeditions. Henderson had gotten him out of trouble on several occasions because of his indebtedness. He also advanced money to Boone at times as the two became personal friends.

Henderson, an astute businessman, devised a scheme whereby he could purchase twenty million acres from the Cherokees (nearly all of present Kentucky and Tennessee). He realized that the British would be involved with the insurrection of the thirteen colonies. Likewise, the Revolutionaries of Virginia would be too involved in war preparations to pay much attention to the project he had planned.

Since the Shawnees had signed a peace treaty with the white man, all that remained to be done was to buy off the Cherokee nation. Henderson was well aware of Boone's knowledge of the Indians and secured his services to work out a treaty.

At Sycamore Shoals on the Watauga River in Tennessee, Boone agreed to pay the Cherokees fifty thousand dollars or its equivalent in goods, for the land east to the mountain barrier that was watered by the Cumberland and Kentucky rivers. It was a total of ninety thousand square miles.

Henderson knew his scheme was illegal and would encounter objections from Governors Dunmore of Virginia and Martin of North Carolina. He hoped, however, that his new territory, which he called Transylvania, would eventually become the fourteenth colony of the Union.

Boone proceeded to work out the treaty and, on the specified day, delivered ten wagon loads of brightly colored shirts, mirrors, ribbons, beads and other trinkets to the Cherokee nation, about twelve hundred Indians in all, led by Chief Attakullaculla. That amounted to about one-fourth cent per acre.

It took several days to complete the deal and even then not all the chiefs were in agreement. Plenty of food was served and only after the bargain was completed on March 1 did Boone bring out the rum.

One young brave was so infuriated about the paltry deal that he told Boone, "Brother, it's good land we have sold you, but you will find it hard to hold."

Chapter 6
Kentucky (1769) West Virginia (1789)

Wilderness--Life and Death Struggle

Henderson's next move was to hire Daniel and his brother, Squire, along with Michael Stoner and thirty other pioneers, including William Hays, Richard Calloway and a few slaves, to blaze a 258-mile trail from Kingsport, Tennessee, to the Kentucky River via the Cumberland Gap. Boone's married daughter, Susannah and a Negro woman were the only females in the group. The trail, which followed a well-trod buffalo trace, was cut barely wide enough for an oxcart to squeeze through. A few small, crude bridges were built along the way and it soon became known as the Wilderness Road.

On March 10, 1775, they began their arduous task which took them through thick marshes, tall canebrakes and heavy underbrush filled with thick, heavy vines. Many trees had to be cut. Boone was to receive two thousand acres for his services and each worker was to receive forty-seven dollars for his labors, which was equivalent to the price of four hundred acres.

One day, while the men were finishing their evening meal near the present Berea, they were fired upon by Indians. Two men were killed during the skirmish. The two women and a few men became so frightened that they returned home.

Boone and the remainder of his party reached the Kentucky River on April 1 and immediately started to build a fort, known as Fort Boonesborough, to protect themselves from marauding Indians.

A site was selected about fifty feet from the river. The exterior was built from large trees placed upright side by side in a rectangular shape. Towers were located at each corner and twenty-six cabins were built inside the walls, which were twelve feet high. A firing deck was attached about seven feet above the ground in the interior of the stockade.

As the fort was nearing completion, Colonel Henderson arrived on April 19, 1775, with his caravan of fifty men, forty pack horses and a few cattle. It was the same day British soldiers in Lexington,

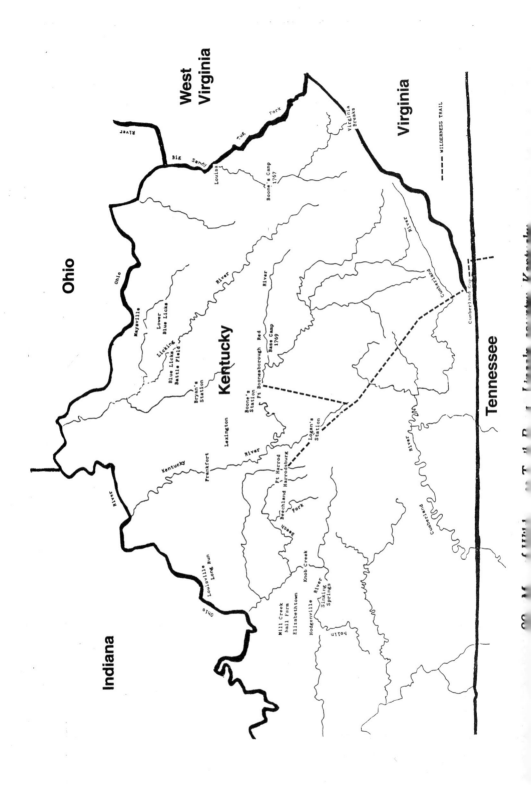

60 Map of Wilderness Road Leading to early Kentucky

23. *Interior of reconstructed Fort Bonnesborough, completed in 1975 (original was constructed by Daniel Boone in 1775), Boonesborough State Park overlooking the Kentucky River eighteen miles south of Lexington, Kentucky.*

Authors birthplace

Hingham

North Wales
Gwynedd
Oley
Exeter T S
Freehold
T S
Clarkesburg

Braddock's Grave
Ft Necessity
Ft Duquesne

Harpers Perry
Antietam
Nancy Hanks
Memorial
Winchester
Washington D C

Philippi 1861

Linville
Creek
Culpeper
Richmond
Williamsburg
Yorktown

Shenandoah Valley
Appomattox
Court House

Beaver Creek
Farmington
Mocksville
Boone
Wilkesboro
Boone's Cave
Ferguson
Brushy Mountains
Cowpens
Salisbury
Battlefield

Ft Detroit

Chillicothe

Point Pleasant
Battle 1774
Virginia Breaks
Castlewood
Cumberland Gap

Kingsport

#

Maysville
Blue Licks
Battlefield
Ft Boonesborough
Harrodsburg
Knob Creek
Beechland
Hodgenville

Long Run
Frankfort
Elizabethtown

Corydon
Rockport
Boonville
Vincennes
Gentryville

Chicago

New Salem
Springfield
Charleston
Goosenest
Prairie
Moore Home
Vandalia

Femme Osage
Dist.
St Louis
Marthasville
Defiance

Massachusetts, tried to seize a colonial depot and were met by a ragtag militia called "the minutemen" who fired the shot heard around the world. That is considered by most Americans to be the first battle of the American Revolution.

It was also about the time the Quakers stopped buying slaves and began freeing those they already owned, setting an example for other colonists to follow.

The first church service held in Kentucky was conducted at Fort Boonesborough on May 28 by the Reverend John Lytle, an Anglican minister. The first baptism there took place a year later. It was also about the time that Joseph Boone (great grandson of George, Sr.) was married to Mary Lincoln (granddaughter of Mordecai, Jr.).

In mid-June, when the fort was finished, Boone returned home for several weeks, where his heart was gladdened to be embraced by his wife, Becky and their children. When he returned to the fort on September 8, he brought Becky and their children with him, along with Squire and his family and Becky's relatives, the Bryans. Becky and Jemima, who was in the very blush of girlhood and innocence, were the first white women to view the Kentucky River from Fort Boonesborough, the first fortified settlement in Kentucky.

By now, two other families of importance had moved into the Kentucky wilderness. Colonel Richard Calloway settled in Fort Boonesborough and Colonel Benjamin Logan built Logans Station.

The pioneers had to be constantly alert. A man could be out plowing his cornfield and a bullet from the gun of a hidden Indian would whiz past his ear. If a pioneer had not secured his cattle at night, he most likely would find the next morning that they had been shot or stolen. The greatest weapon the Indians possessed was fear created in the pioneer settlements. Every cracking of a twig, especially at night, produced fear anew.

Small skirmishes with the Indians were taking place daily. Death by the tomahawk and the scalping knife had become common in the wilderness. Two days before Christmas, two young boys had crossed the river and were attacked by Indians. One was scalped and later died. The other boy was never found. That created such a panic that, out of the original five hundred settlers, only two hundred remained at the fort by July 4, 1776, the day the colonists declared their independence from England.

The British needed allies badly and the Indians, located west of the mountain barrier, were a convenient natural choice, just as they had been with the French during the French and Indian War about fifteen years earlier. For the next six years, Lieutenant Governor Hamilton in Fort Detroit furnished food, guns and ammunition to the red man, as well as leadership. He still paid a bounty for each scalp taken from a paleface. Hamilton soon became known as the "hair buyer." This was a union of the bayonet and the tomahawk. The red man now felt he had a powerful friend at his back. The colonists were struggling for their independence and the British were striving to crush the rebellion.

The British seemed unable to recognize that the pioneers west of the mountain barrier might have welcomed them as allies to help fight the Indians. Many pioneers were Tories still loyal to the crown, including Becky's relatives who had built Bryan's Station sixteen miles north of Boonesborough. That oversight could very well have cost them the war. The settlers needed help in fighting the Indians, not an additional foe.

At that time, the colonists had more than they could handle just looking after their own safety, without paying much attention to the frontier. Although a reinforcement for the fort was expected momentarily, it did not arrive until several months later.

Life at Boonesborough was beginning to settle down to a routine of hunting, farming, rendering salt and weaving cloth. It was evident that some rules were needed to regulate the activities of the people. A council, the first in Kentucky, was called on May 23. In attendance were Daniel and Squire, Colonel Calloway and John Floyd. Colonel Henderson presided.

Daniel was given credit for two of the nine laws that were passed. One was designed to preserve the game supply and the other to improve the breed of horses. Another bill was presented to prevent profanity and Sabbath-breaking. Not everyone agreed entirely with the laws that were passed. The session lasted three days and ended, as it had begun, with the celebration of a divine service and baptism with Reverend Lytle officiating.

There were now four settlements in Kentucky: Boonesborough, Harrodsburg, Boiling Springs and Logans Station. All were represented at the council meeting. These settlements were populated with people still subjects of England, since the news of the battle at Lexington had not reached the outposts.

Things were happening back in the colonies that were newsworthy to the pioneers: the restriction of slave trade; the heavy taxation of slave trade to prevent its spread; and the removal of authority the Anglican Churches had enjoyed while being tax-supported throughout the colonies. One bit of news from Rockingham County, Virginia, was the promotion of Abraham Lincoln (grandfather of the sixteenth president) to the rank of captain in the militia. He was to be called Captain the remainder of his life.

Things had gone fairly well for a time in the settlements because the Indians had taken little action against the pioneers. However, it proved to be the calm before the storm. On Sunday afternoon July 14, three teenage girls--Betsy Calloway, sixteen, her sister, Fanny and Jemima Boone, both fourteen--were enjoying a leisurely canoe ride on the river not far from the fort. The canoe drifted close to the embankment on the far side of the river. The girls were seized and taken captive by five fierce-looking Indians. During the initial scuffle, while the girls were trying to escape, Betsy hit one Indian over the head with a paddle.

The Indians headed north at a fast pace with their captives. Betsy tried throughout the ordeal to console the two younger girls while causing her captors as much trouble as possible, hoping this would allow the men from the fort to overtake them. She sank her heels into the soft ground and tore off pieces of her dress to leave a trail for the rescue party to follow.

Their captors seemed proud of the young girls they had captured. They envisioned the handsome trophy the girls would make while being put on parade through the Shawnee village. That gave the Indians an incentive to return to their village as quickly as possible and a route by way of Blue Licks was chosen.

Captain Boone and Colonel Calloway were away the night the alarm was sounded at the fort. They returned early the next morning and formed two search parties, one led by Boone and the other by Calloway, the father of the two sisters. It was considered imperative that at least one of the rescue parties reach the Ohio River before the Indians.

Boone decided to take his group on a more direct route to the river, even though it was rougher terrain, where he suspected the

Indians would be crossing. All the while, the girls behaved so badly that they slowed the progress of the Indians considerably. Boone and his group actually crossed over their trail several times while in pursuit.

On the morning of the third day, Boone and his party came upon the Indian encampment. They saw Betsy sitting on the ground near a tree, consoling the younger girls by holding their heads in her lap. The young braves were busily preparing a buffalo roast, each performing a separate chore of gathering wood, tending the fire or roasting the meat. At any rate, the girls did not appear to be guarded by any Indian in particular because all of the Indians' weapons were lying on the ground.

Boone was more interested in the safety of the girls than any harm he might do to their captors. A plan of rescue was agreed upon whereby each man would pick a target, fire his rifle and, at the same time, rush the encampment to rescue the girls. As the shots were fired, one brave grabbed his tomahawk and threw it at the girls, barely missing Betsy's head. She had moved just enough to prevent the weapon from finding its mark and it stuck into the tree behind them. Jemima jumped up, screaming, "That's Daddy!"

The son of Chief Blackfish was shot and fell forward into the fire, but he managed to stagger away into the woods. Only one other of the five escaped. The men were so elated about rescuing the three frightened girls, they made no effort at pursuit. It should be remembered that Boone never killed an Indian or an animal for the sport of it.

A month had gone by since the daring rescue when Betsy Calloway and Samuel Henderson, a younger brother of Colonel Henderson, celebrated the occasion by getting married. A festive affair was prepared, with Squire officiating at the fort's first wedding. Everyone at the fort attended.

The colonel spared no expense and provided a feast of wild and tame meat, wild turkey, hot biscuits, blackberry cobbler and all the trimmings to round out the fare. The fiddlers were kept busy into the wee hours of the morning. They played good old mountain music while the celebrants danced to their hearts' content. Finally, Betsy and Samuel climbed the wooden ladder to the sleeping loft. Betsy's mother had made a new mattress of corn shucks for this special occasion.

Colonel Henderson had the only store in Kentucky at that time and he charged outrageous prices for his merchandise. He was also getting a whopping thirteen and one-half cents for an acre. Everyone assumed he owned the fort and all the land for miles in any direction and he was getting away with it. The pioneers were furious at being forced to pay such exorbitant prices for the necessities of life. Some satisfaction came on December 31 when Kentucky County was created out of the southwestern part of Virginia and all Transylvania Company land, including Boonesborough, was taken over by the county.

Two years later, Henderson's land title was declared null and void. The State of Virginia later gave Henderson 200,000 acres in Kentucky to compensate him for his part in helping to establish the first white man's fortified settlement in Kentucky. Boone also lost title to his two thousand acres, but he was not compensated for his efforts.

On September 20, good news reached the fort that on Christmas Eve, 1776, General Washington and his group of ragtag, ill-shod soldiers had crossed the Delaware during a violent snow and sleet storm. This daring venture had a great effect on the morale of his men and the patriots in the colonies. That great feat resulted in an early morning surprise attack on the mercenary German Hessians, who were asleep. They had been in bed only a short time, trying to sober up from an all-night Christmas Eve celebration.

About forty Hessians were killed or wounded and more than one thousand taken prisoner. Washington's small army suffered only six casualties, including two who froze to death on the march. That was a much-needed and glorious victory for the colonists.

During the year, Spain and France recognized the United States as an independent country and declared war on England. A Frenchman, Marquis de Lafayette, twenty, was very helpful to the colonists' cause in securing an alliance between France and the newly recognized country.

Boone was concerned because Becky's relatives, the Bryans, were Tory sympathizers and her brother was fighting for the redcoats. Nevertheless, Becky always remained loyal to her husband.

In Virginia, Thomas Lincoln (Abe's father), the third son of Captain Abraham, was born on January 6, 1778, on Linville Creek in Rockingham County. Joseph Boone (Squire's nephew) married Nancy Lincoln (a sister of Thomas). Boone's mother (Sarah Morgan Boone) died in Mocksville, North Carolina and was buried beside her husband in the Joppa Cemetery.

On February 2, Boone led a group of men to Blue Licks on a salt-rendering expedition. It took 840 gallons of boiled-down salt brine to make one bushel of salt. Many bushels of salt were used at the fort to cure meat for winter.

For several days, while the other men were rendering salt, Boone was in the woods hunting game for their food supply. He had hunted all day and was on his way back to camp when he was surrounded by about one hundred armed Shawnees. Since there was no way to escape, he extended his hand in friendship to Chief Blackfish. He pretended to be a friend and loyal to the British, who were allied with the Indians throughout the Revolution. Boone always remained calm under the most stressful situations.

During the ensuing conversation, he learned that the Shawnees were on their way to capture Fort Boonesborough. Boone knew the fort did not have enough men to defend against an attack and everyone would either be killed or captured. Those captured would be forced to walk several hundred miles to Fort Detroit in deep snow and freezing weather. Many women and children would surely perish on the forced march.

Boone was in the difficult position of trying to be friendly with the Indians and protect his own people at the same time. A single hasty or false step, however slight, would betray all. From that precarious position, he made a proposal to the chief, telling him it would be difficult to capture the fort at this time because it was heavily fortified with men and ammunition. It also would be impossible to transport the women and children to Detroit under such severe weather conditions. Boone suggested they wait until spring and then he personally would go with them, as a friend, to capture the fort.

Chief Blackfish felt that was an acceptable proposal but still wanted to capture the other men at the salt lick. Boone reasoned further with the chief. He would lead them to the other men, who would not resist, if the chief would agree to their safety and humane treatment, which included not having to run the torturous Indian gauntlet. It was agreed and sealed with a handshake between the two great men and, throughout Boone's captivity, Blackfish kept his part of the agreement to the letter.

The Shawnees had great respect for Boone. To them, he was the courageous leader of the white man in Kentucky. They considered him trustworthy and, above all, never inhumane, because he never killed without being forced to do so by circumstances beyond his control. The chief, his braves and their captive then proceeded to the salt lick where Boone signaled for the men to surrender without a fight.

Chief Blackfish started for the Shawnee village at Chillicothe on February 18 with his prize catch. Boone was very hurt because his men thought him a traitor due to his friendly actions toward the Indians. But Boone knew if he did not pretend to be a friend to his captors, he and his men and their loved ones at the fort would be killed.

The salt renderers were taken to Fort Detroit and sold to the British. Boone also wanted to be sold. He tried to make a deal with Governor Hamilton, promising that if he were bought he would remain a loyal subject of King George of England. The governor offered the Shawnees five hundred dollars for his release, but the chief was so fond of Boone that he refused the offer.

Blackfish naively thought that he could, in time, induce Boone to accept the Shawnees as brothers by adopting him as a son--possibly to replace the son who had been killed recently. The chief did know that Boone could teach the braves many of the white man's ways.

Back at the Shawnee village, Boone went through a lengthy ritual to become a Shawnee. They plucked out all of his hair except a small tuft on top of his head. The young women scrubbed him with sand and dunked him in the creek to remove all traces of white blood and then he was accepted as a son of Blackfish. To show his appreciation and delight, the chief gave him a pretty maiden as his wife.

Boone dared not refuse the gift for fear it would insult his newly acquired brothers. She cooked and sewed for him and kept the tepee neat and clean. In return, Boone brought her fresh game and treated her with respect. He did have a problem with the possibility he might create jealousy between himself and the young braves. Therefore, he always managed to be the poorest marksman in a shooting contest and the weakest in feats requiring physical strength. He even considered it wise to applaud their war dances and did so with enthusiasm.

While Boone was being held captive by the Shawnees, George Rogers Clark, brother of William Clark of the Lewis and Clark expedition, planned an invasion of the Northwest to capture several British posts.

Simon Kenton and others from Fort Boonesborough volunteered to help Clark in his endeavor. The expedition was a great success. A total eclipse of the sun aided them while they ran the Ohio Falls, enabling them to surprise the British at Vincennes, Indiana. After two days and nights of fighting, Governor Hamilton and his men surrendered.

Back at the village, Blackfish trusted his adopted son so much that he talked freely with his warriors in Boone's presence about plans to capture Fort Boonesborough. All the while, Boone pretended to be unconcerned.

The braves were too proud to do menial work and left the salt-making to Boone and the women, which created a good relationship. He gained valuable knowledge about Indian habits, their thinking and their way of life, which was to be useful to him in the future.

The tribe allowed him to hunt alone, but he was to bring back game for each bullet fired. Boone reasoned that by cutting each bullet in half and using just half as much powder, he could still get a piece of game and save the remainder for when he escaped.

At dawn on June 16, a flock of wild turkeys were heard gobbling some distance from the village. Within a few minutes, all of the young braves had rushed out in pursuit. Very calmly, Boone watched them as they disappeared into the forest. The women, and especially the young one who had shared his tepee for the past five months and had developed a deep feeling for him, knew immediately what his thoughts were.

Now was the chance he had been waiting for so patiently, and he knew every second would count as he picked up his rifle, mounted his horse and rode into the woods, where he retrieved his hidden cache of gunpowder, bullets and a small piece of dried venison. Then he reined his horse into a small stream and followed it the first day, leaving no tracks for the Indians to follow.

Boone, now forty-two, knew it was a matter of life or death, so he pushed his horse to the limit. After several hours of hard riding, his horse gave out. He continued for another two-and one-half days on foot, traveling 160 miles and stopping only once for a meal.

When he reached the Ohio River, it was at flood stage, but he was blessed with a bit of luck by finding an abandoned canoe. He took a few minutes to make necessary repairs, then he used it to cross the swollen river. In the early morning of the fourth day, he staggered into the fort, resembling an Indian so much that his brothers, Israel and Squire, barely recognized him. He learned from them that Becky had taken the family back to her father's place in the Yadkin Valley, believing that Daniel had been killed by his captors.

As the settlers gathered around, he heard a familiar voice, turned around and saw his daughter, Jemima, pushing toward him with outstretched arms. She had stayed behind with her fiance, Flanders Calloway. Jemima, who was not really his own child, was the only one of his family who was there to greet him.

Good news had filtered into the fort about George Rogers Clark, who had taken three British posts: Kaskaskia, Cahokia and Vincennes. In addition, the French fleet and land troops had joined the colonists in their desperate struggle against the English.

Boone found the fort badly in need of repairs and, even worse, there were only fifty men to defend it. Knowing the plans of the Shawnees, he set about making the fort as safe as possible in the short amount of time they had.

On September 6, Chief Blackfish, accompanied by 444 warriors and twelve French Canadians, including De Quindre and his slave, Pompey, arrived at the fort. They approached the gate under a white flag of truce carried by Pompey. They had been hoping that Boone had returned to the fort and would surrender it as he had promised.

Boone walked through the gate and was greeted warmly by Chief Blackfish, who cried as he asked, "Why did you abandon us?"

"I wanted to see my wife and children so badly that I couldn't stay away any longer."

"Had I known," Blackfish said, "I would have let you go any time and would have aided you in any way I could."

Blackfish said he had brought forty horses to transport the women and children from the fort. Boone then asked for a two-day truce, at which point the braves reminded him of his promise to help them take the fort. He replied that the decision would be left up to the people at the fort.

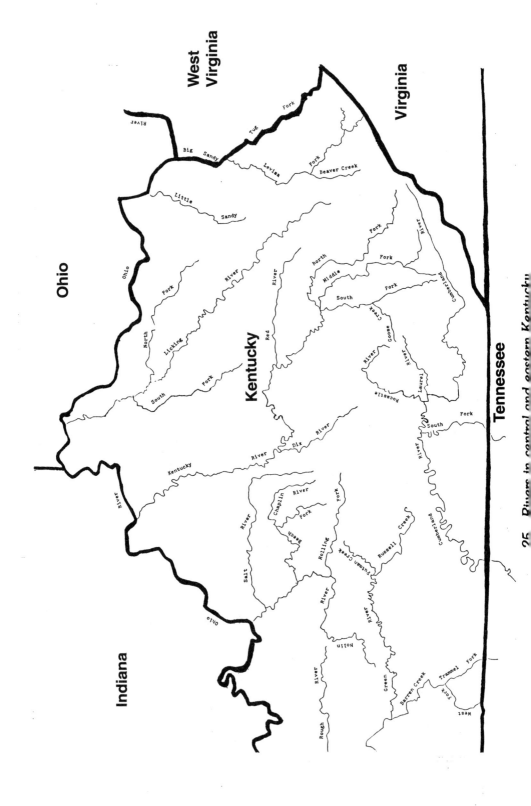

25. Rivers in central and eastern Kentucky

While the fort's leaders were planning their strategy, they also were preparing the fort for an imminent siege. They brought in as much corn and water as they thought they could without arousing the suspicion of the Indians. They also brought in their horses and cattle.

On the third day, Boone and nine others met again with the Indians outside the stockade. He told the chief that the fort's inhabitants preferred death to captivity and would not surrender. The Indians then pretended they wanted to agree to a treaty anyway by shaking hands to bind the agreement.

Boone knew it was a ruse and waved his hand as a signal for the men in the stockade to commence firing. The ten men then ran back through the gate and only Squire was wounded.

For eight terrible days and nights, the fifty men and their families at the fort, plus those at the three other Kentucky settlements, were under heavy siege. The Indians used every tactic at their disposal. The forest rang again and again with their shrill screams. If the Indians had known about scaling ladders, they could have poured their fierce warriors into the fort at will. Since they did not know about such ladders, it gave the pioneers a small hope of surviving.

It literally rained bullets as the young braves fired at will. Others repeatedly rushed the fort with lighted torches and flaming arrows were shot to set fire to cabin roofs within the stockade. The men, women and children worked desperately around the clock to prevent their massacre. The men carefully picked their targets and made each shot count to conserve their meager supply of ammunition, while the women stood behind them and reloaded the rifles.

On the seventh day of the siege, the Indians began to dig a tunnel, starting at the river bank, which they hoped would lead them to the interior of the stockade. The muddy river water gave away their plan and the men at the fort started to dig a tunnel of their own inside the fort to intersect the one being dug by the Indians.

Food, water and ammunition were now at a desperately low level. The sanitary conditions were beyond description. It was feared that the Indians would break through the stockade walls at any moment and all of the inhabitants then would be tortured and brutally put to death by the tomahawk.

The eighth day of the siege began with a torrential rain which put out the remaining fires in the cabins. It also began to erode the walls of the tunnel, which was nearing completion.

To the great surprise and joy of the weary people inside the stockade, the Indians suddenly gave up the siege and departed, taking with them thirty-seven known dead. The fort, surprisingly, had lost only two men, with five others wounded. Jemima had been wounded in the buttock, which proved embarrassing when the bullet was being removed. Thus ended the longest and most ferocious Indian siege in Kentucky and the last major attack on Fort Boonesborough.

Just one more day of assault by the Indians and the people at the fort would have surrendered because of the lack of food and water and from complete exhaustion. It seemed evident to them that the hand of the Master was there again. Before leaving, the Indians destroyed all of the corn in the fields and the hogs that were running loose in the woods, leaving the pioneers with almost no food.

If the fort had fallen, settling Kentucky would have been put off for many years. During the repair of the fort, about 125 pounds of lead was collected from the stockade walls and melted down to make bullets.

Boone had saved Boonesborough, but before he could go to North Carolina to bring his family back to Kentucky, he was requested to appear before a military court at Logans Station, with Colonel Benjamin Logan presiding. He was charged with treason for betraying the men who were captured at the salt lick and with cooperating with the British and the Indians.

The charges were brought by Colonel Richard Calloway (uncle of Jemima's soon-to-be husband, Flanders Calloway). Colonel Calloway was jealous of Captain Boone because often he was obliged to take orders from him, though Captain Boone held a lesser rank.

Boone was embarrassed when he appeared in court to relate the facts of the case. It was noted that not one man captured at the salt lick had been killed. Boone was cleared of all charges and promoted to major in the Virginia Militia for services beyond the call of duty.

One day, Major Boone and a few other men were caught outside the fort by marauding Indians. They were cut off from the stockade gate and were heavily outnumbered. Boone gave the order to charge and he and six other men fell wounded. A young brave raised his tomahawk and was ready to bury it in Boone's skull when, just in the nick of time, Simon Kenton shot the brave and managed to carry Boone toward the stockade.   As he approached the fort, Jemima assisted in the rescue.

Kenton, Boone's close friend, was one of the greatest Indian fighters of all times.   He had been forced to run the Indian gauntlet on eight different occasions and was fastened spread-eagle to the stake three times for several days of torture from the hot sun and biting ants.

When Boone returned to the Yadkin Valley, his wife and children shouted with joy to see that he was still alive.   They thought he had been killed by the Shawnees after he and the other men had been captured at the salt lick.   Becky was reluctant to return to Kentucky for awhile because of the treason trial, her Tory relatives, and the tales she had heard about the young woman her husband had lived with while in captivity.

It was during this time that Chief Blackfish was wounded in a skirmish at Chillicothe and did not recover.

Within the year, Boone returned to Kentucky with Becky and the children, but because the treason trial left such an unhappy memory, he did not stay long at the fort.

In 1779, Daniel and his brothers, Samuel and George, moved their families five miles to a spot on the north side of the Kentucky River where he built a large cabin known as Boones Station.   He returned to the fort only when necessary or in time of trouble.

Boonesborough became the first town chartered in Kentucky and the first school in Kentucky opened there that same year.   Joseph Doniphan held classes with only one book, the Bible and a few leaves from a hymnal.   The children wrote with pens made from goose feathers and ink made from pokeberries.

When the Legislature in Richmond declared Colonel Henderson's scheme illegal, everyone who had land claims with the company was supposed to pay a fee and register their claims with the State of Virginia.   Otherwise, swindlers might register claims and the settlers would lose their land.

Boone had his own claims for five thousand acres, so he took those and the claims of all of the others around Boonesborough and started for Richmond to fulfill the state's requirements.   To everyone's surprise, he returned home within a few days. He had been waylaid and robbed of twenty thousand dollars belonging to the pioneers. Some of those who had trusted Boone with their money accused him of stealing it.

This was a trying time for him: first his loyalty had been challenged and now his honesty. Many years later, Boone managed to repay everyone the money he had lost. The Virginia land law was a very poor one and Boone was one of the first victims to be turned out of his home because he could not prove ownership.

Two happy events took place at Boonesborough early in 1780. Flanders Calloway and Jemima Boone were married. Flanders's uncle, Colonel Calloway, performed the ceremony. Julia Boone (a distant cousin of Daniel's) became the bride of Mordecai Lincoln (a grandson of Mordecai, Jr.).

The Indians waited daily for a chance to surprise the pioneers, shooting from ambush while the settlers were working in the corn fields or hunting in the woods for game. This kept them in constant fear. One day, while Colonel Calloway was cutting a tree to make a canoe, he was shot and killed by an Indian.

Even though Ned was the father of Jemima, he was Daniel's constant companion. The brothers often traveled together to the salt licks. While rendering salt one day, they were ambushed by Indians. The heavy fire of the braves was fatal to Ned. They cut off his head and took it with them, thinking it was Daniel's.

Daniel was heavily outnumbered. He was forced to abandon his brother and run for his life or face the same fate. The warriors soon turned from mutilation of the dead to chase the living. Daniel ran more than three miles to escape the Indians but was unable to outrun a vicious dog they had put on his trail. When he was nearly exhausted, he stopped the dog's progress with an unerring rifle shot and made his escape.

Daniel had lost the brother who meant the most to him and it was very difficult for him to accept Ned's death. For several years, he kept a supply of meat on the table of Ned's widow, Martha, who was Becky's younger sister.

Boone was promoted to the rank of lieutenant colonel, became sheriff of Fayette County, a deputy surveyor and a member of the House of Burgesses in Richmond. While attending to his legislative duties, he met and worked with Governor Thomas Jefferson and Patrick Henry, another legislator.

Whether in battle or at home, captive or free, Colonel Boone was always a firm but gentle man. He never used his power with wanton cruelty and the kind treatment of him by the Indians when he was their captive confirms this. They knew him as a foe, but a generous and brave one.

A bit of sad news from the colonies had filtered into the wilderness of Kentucky, telling about a couple of setbacks for the American Revolutionary cause.   On May 12, 1780, at Charleston, South Carolina, General Benjamin Lincoln was forced to surrender his entire army of 2,500 men, practically all of the regular army south of the Potomac. To make matters worse, another contingent of the American Army, under the leadership of General Lafayette, had to retreat before the advancing British Army and Navy led by turncoat Benedict Arnold.

Boone's third trip to Pennsylvania, in early October 1781, was his first since Braddock's defeat at Fort Duquesne in 1755 and its capture in 1757. He was unaware that the revolution was about to come to an end for the territory east of the Appalachians when he, Becky and their young son, Nathan, rode horseback to Exeter Township. There they visited his birthplace and many of his relatives and friends, including the Lincolns who had remained there. Thomas Lincoln, later in life, told of hearing Boone describe his many adventures in the wilds of Kentucky.

During that visit, the war came to an end east of the mountains. Some textbooks state that Lord Cornwallis surrendered at Yorktown. Although his army did surrender, Lord Cornwallis was such a proud man that some historians believe he feigned an illness and remained in bed.   Therefore, he sent General Charles O'Hara to handle the capitulation for the British.

General O'Hara, in trying to embarrass General Washington, first offered Lord Cornwallis's sword to Rochambeau, the French commander, who refused it, saying, "General Washington should receive it." O'Hara then offered the sword to Washington, who also refused it, saying, "General Benjamin Lincoln is to receive the sword of Lord Cornwallis," thus signifying the British cessation on October 19, 1781.   Since General Lincoln had earlier suffered the shame of surrender to Cornwallis at Charleston, he was distinguished by

Washington with the honor of receiving the sword from O'Hara. General Lincoln later became secretary of war (1781-84).

After the surrender, Washington went home to see his wife, Martha, whom he had not seen for quite awhile. He wanted very much to show his great appreciation to General Lafayette, so he invited him to visit his home at Mt. Vernon.

Lafayette placed his life and fortune at the disposal of the fighting American colonists in 1777 and served without pay. Congress gave him the rank of major general and placed him directly under General Washington's command.

Lafayette was instrumental in inducing the French government to sign a Treaty of Alliance with the colonies in 1778. Without that, the colonists probably would not have won the war. He was also a main factor, along with the aid of Rochambeau's land army and De Grasse's naval fleet, in the final defeat and surrender of Cornwallis's army.

It was the second Sunday in November when Washington and Lafayette attended the morning service at Christ Church in Alexandria. Afterward, they stood on either side of the exit and shook hands and conversed as the congregation slowly made its departure. This was a long affair because most war news was by word-of-mouth and everyone wanted to hear details of the victory from someone of authority.

As one account goes, after a great length of time, vivacious Lucy Hanks, sixteen, emerged on the side where Lafayette was doing the greeting. He seemed attracted to Lucy because he not only shook her hand, he also kissed her. A wealthy young Virginia planter, who was a bachelor and an Oxford student, observed with great interest when Lucy was kissed.

Lucy's family had been neighbors of the Boone and Lincoln families in Berks County about thirty years earlier. They left the area about the same time and built a log cabin located between the Potomac and Rappahannock rivers in Fairfax County, Virginia.

Early Tuesday morning, the young planter, in high spirits, rode horseback to the Hanks' cabin and knocked at the door. Lucy answered it. He inquired if she would be interested in being employed at his plantation. Lucy was thrilled with the chance to earn money, because hers was an illiterate but decent family living in a cabin with a dirt floor.

He did not give Lucy an "easy" job, such as working in the fields with the slaves or in the kitchen cooking or washing the dishes. He gave her a "hard" task, which was dusting the furniture with a feather duster.

One day, when walking through the library, he found Lucy gently dusting and simultaneously looking at pictures in a history book.

He asked Lucy, "Would you like to learn to read and write?"

With enthusiasm, she said, "Yes!"

At that time, Virginia had no free schools and a family who wished to send a child to a private school surely would not send a second-class female citizen. And it was unheard of for a servant girl to aspire to learn to read and write.

As time passed, Lucy learned to read and write. One thing led to another, especially at night, while sitting around an open fire and it was easy for her to fall in love with her tutor.

It was inevitable that one day Lucy would discover she was pregnant. For several weeks she was in agony, not knowing what to do. Finally, when she could no longer hide it, she told the father. Lucy was then given some money and eased out the back door to return home. For a young lady to be with child out of wedlock was, at that time, most disgraceful. The identity of Lucy's lover was never disclosed, but it can be assumed her family knew. Whether it was from great love, respect, shame or plain stubbornness, it was indeed kept a secret.

The burden was heavy for Lucy and her family. Her family withstood the embarrassment and humiliation as long as they could. Then they moved about one hundred miles into the wilderness to Mineral County, Virginia (now West Virginia), located seven-and one-half miles up Mikes Run from Antioch along the present Highway 50. Lucy's father, Joseph Hanks, had built a two-room cabin there.

It was there, on February 4, 1783, that baby Nancy's life in the world began. Lucy was assisted by her mother and sisters. Nancy was born in an area where Indians were still a menace. However, she was surrounded by a loving mother, three doting aunts and other family members. She was, no doubt, the most comfortable member of the family. There was wood for the fireplace, good spring water nearby and meat from wild game for the table.

26. Reconstructed birthplace of Nancy Hanks (mother of President Abraham Lincoln), born here February 4, 1783 located 7½ miles up Mike's Run from Antioch, along Highway 50, in northeastern West Virginia in Mineral County. Nancy was born illegitimate. Her father was a second generation Virginia

The Virginia Enumerator dated September 24, 1782, was incorporated into the U.S. census of 1790. It showed the Hanks family as new residents at that time. Eighty-one years later, on June 20, 1863, President Lincoln signed a bill declaring West Virginia a separate state.

In a biography of Lincoln written by William H. Herndon, who was Lincoln's law partner for twenty-one years, the following quote appears on pages three and four in the first volume:

"On the subject of his ancestry and origin, I only remember one time when Mr. Lincoln ever referred to it. It was about 1850, when he and I were driving in his one-horse buggy to the court in Menard County, Illinois. The suit we were going to try was one in which we were likely to touch upon the subject of hereditary traits. During the ride he spoke, for the first time in my hearing, of his mother, dealing on her characteristics and mentioning or enumerating what qualities he inherited from her.

"He said among other things, that she was the daughter of Lucy Hanks and a well-bred but obscure Virginia farmer or planter; and he argued that from this last source came his power of analysis, his logic, his mental activity, his ambition and all the qualities that distinguished him from the other members and descendants of the Hanks family."

Years later, when Lucy's grandson, President Lincoln, was asked about the identity of his grandfather on his mother's side, his reply was, "I believe he was a planter and his ancestors were second families of Virginia."

When baby Nancy was about nine months old, her grandfather, Joseph Hanks, and his family left Mikes Run and migrated to North Carolina where they met the Boone and Lincoln families again. At the same time, Captain Abraham Lincoln, son of Virginia John, moved his family from Linville Creek, Virginia, to North Carolina, in preparation for migrating to Kentucky. Boone had encouraged him to do so when he had visited him two years earlier.

At that time, Boone organized his last family group to migrate to Kentucky. In this group was Captain Lincoln and his wife, Bathsheba, and their three sons, including Thomas, five years old, and two daughters. In this same group was Joseph Hanks and his family, including Lucy and her baby, Nancy.

There is little doubt that it was the close association with Boone that influenced the Lincoln and Hanks families to move to Kentucky. Boone had told them about the black, rich soil, the blue grass, the tall timber in forests full of game and the clear water loaded with fish.

The migration of the two families, along with others, through the Cumberland Gap following the Wilderness Trail, was uneventful other than the usual hardships of the times. Captain Lincoln and family first settled at Mill Creek, seven miles north of Elizabethtown, Kentucky, in Hardin County. Two years later, they moved to Long Run, located about ten miles east of present Louisville in Jefferson County.

Boone previously had selected and surveyed the four hundred acres which Captain Lincoln bought. The Hanks family settled in Mercer County near Fort Harrod where they might have assumed no one knew them. Strangers might have thought Nancy's father was killed during the war.

Along the eastern seaboard, the Revolution had been won, but in the back country the war raged on more fiercely than ever. The British had surrendered their colonies, but they hoped they could still prevent the loss of the Ohio and Mississippi river valleys. Toward that end, they enticed the Indians to be more ruthless than ever in their attacks against the pioneers.

Simon Girty, the white traitor who lived with the Indians, came with a force of five hundred warriors to attack Bryans Station which had been built by Becky's relatives. Colonel John Todd, the officer of highest rank, formed an expedition for revenge. Colonel Trigg had received word that Colonel Logan and 154 men were coming to reinforce them but were a day's journey away.

Lieutenant Colonel Boone advised Colonel Todd to delay until Colonel Logan and his men could join them, because he calculated the Indian force to be about five hundred. The Indians left a trail so plainly marked that Lieutenant Colonel Boone knew it was a trap. The pioneers wanted blood revenge with not one day of delay. Colonel Todd refused to listen to Boone, perhaps out of fear of losing stature with his men.

One young officer, Major Hugh McGary, said, "We don't have time to wait for old ladies." As he rode headlong into the stream, he shouted, "All those who are not cowards, follow me!"

The soldiers dashed madly after him.   Todd, Trigg and Boone followed, trying desperately to bring order out of the chaos.   As Boone suspected, Girty had set a trap and the slaughter took place in short order.   More than seventy-five men were killed, captured or missing, including Boone's young son, Israel, who was mortally wounded in the fighting on August 19, 1782.

Boone was the only commander to come out alive.   It was the darkest day in his life as he picked up his son in his arms and carried him away.   Israel died before reaching the river.   Daniel hid his son's body in a cave and swam the river to safety.

Three days later, the pioneers returned to bury the dead.   They had been scalped by the Indians and preyed on by wolves and vultures to such an extent they were not recognizable.   They were buried in a common grave.   Daniel retrieved Israel's body from the cave and took it to Boones Station for burial beside Ned.   The Blue Licks Battle is considered to be the last battle of the American Revolution.

Before the end of September, General George Rogers Clark and Colonel Boone led a detachment of one thousand men into Chillicothe, the stronghold of the Shawnees and burned everything to the ground.   That was the village where Daniel was held captive for six months.   One of those killed in the raid was Big Jim, the Indian who had tortured young James Boone to death in Powell Valley nine years earlier.

It seemed ironic that the pioneers put their lives on the line, lost many of their loved ones in Indian fighting, went through privation and hardship, defended the land against a thousand perils, yet ended up losing it all.   Boone could not understand the justice of making a set of complicated paper forms superior to the honest and courageous enterprise it took to occupy and settle the wilderness.

He probably could have had all of Kentucky just for the taking.   As it was, he did not own one foot of land to leave to his children.   Confused land claims, sloppy filing procedures and overlapping boundaries gave shrewd land seekers the opportunity to preempt the pioneers' holdings.   The pioneers were then trespassing on their own property.

Becky's relatives lost Bryan Station; Daniel lost Boones Station; and Simon Kenton, the great Indian fighter, was stripped of all of his property and ended up in debtors prison. George Rogers Clark lost all of his land and ended his days as an alcoholic.

Boone, having lost almost everything, moved his wife and family to Maysville (Limestone) where they ran a tavern and store. Becky cooked for men from the flatboats that traveled up and down the Ohio River.

In May 1786, Captain Lincoln was working in his cornfield a short distance from his log cabin at Long Run when an Indian shot him from ambush. He fell mortally wounded at young Tom's feet. Tom's older brother, Mordecai, ran to the cabin and grabbed his father's loaded rifle. He aimed it through a loophole in the cabin wall and fired at the Indian, who was running into the woods with young Tom under his arm. The bullet found its mark and, as the Indian stumbled forward, he dropped Tom, who ran back to the cabin.

Shortly after her husband was killed, Bathsheba moved her family to Beech Fork, in Washington County, less than a mile from Richard Berry's home and eighteen miles west of Fort Harrod, where the Hanks were living.

Bathsheba's oldest son, Mordecai, according to custom, inherited the Lincoln farm when he reached the age of majority and his mother moved to the Mill Creek farm near Elizabethtown. When he was older, Tom went out on his own. He worked as a hired hand while he learned the carpentry trade in Joseph Hanks's shop at Elizabethtown.

The Hanks' move to Kentucky did not bring instant happiness. Hard times and trouble were constant companions. Lucy's quandary was by no means over. She was still quite as pretty and attractive to the men and, over a period of time, she was indicted by the grand jury more than once for fornication.

In November, the sheriff, who knew Lucy, stuck the summons in his pocket and went hunting. In March the following year, the court met again and a female busybody, Ann McGinty, appeared with further gossip and demanded the "hussy" be hauled into court and made to answer to the charges. When the summons was delivered, high-spirited Lucy tore it up and threw it into the face of the man who served it.

Lucy doubtless would have received more citations and been hauled into court if it had not been for Henry Sparrow, who truly loved her. He took out a license on April 26, and they were married a year later.

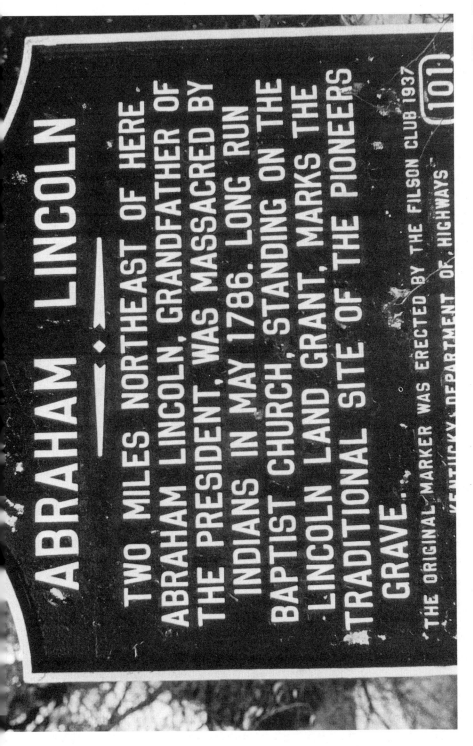

ABRAHAM LINCOLN

TWO MILES NORTHEAST OF HERE ABRAHAM LINCOLN, GRANDFATHER OF THE PRESIDENT, WAS MASSACRED BY INDIANS IN MAY 1786. LONG RUN BAPTIST CHURCH, STANDING ON THE LINCOLN LAND GRANT, MARKS THE TRADITIONAL SITE OF THE PIONEERS GRAVE.

THE ORIGINAL MARKER WAS ERECTED BY THE FILSON CLUB 1937 KENTUCKY DEPARTMENT OF HIGHWAYS

101

27. Captain Abraham Lincoln was born in Berks County, Pennsylvania, in 1744. He lived in Linville Creek, Virginia from 1750 to 1783. He and his wife, Bathsheba Herring, and their family were guided through the Cumberland Gap to Kentucky by Daniel Boone, who had previously surveyed 400 acres of land on Long Run for Captain Lincoln.

Lucy had requested a year's delay so she could clear her name. Sparrow was a Revolutionary War veteran and was at the surrender in Yorktown in 1781. Over the years, he and Lucy had eight children and two of them became preachers.

One of Lucy's grandsons, the son of her illegitimate daughter, became the sixteenth president of the United States. Lucy now lived an exemplary life and became noted for her piety, intelligence, ability to read and write and for her strong and gracious personality. The missteps of her youth were completely forgotten at Fort Harrod where she and her family lived and died.

Boone became unhappy with his situation at Maysville and moved to Point Pleasant in 1787. He built a cabin at the mouth of Campbell Creek near the site of the first battle of the American Revolution in 1774, in which he had taken part. He and Becky ran a store for a short time. It was from here that Daniel and Becky made their final trip back to Pennsylvania to visit friends and relatives. Colonel Boone was elected a representative to the Virginia Legislature from Kanawha County.

Before Nancy's mother, Lucy, married Henry Sparrow, Nancy had gone to live with her Aunt Betsy Sparrow and her husband, Tom. Nancy was happy in her foster home, because her aunt and uncle were the kindest of parents and became her dearest friends.

Nancy grew to be a slender young woman of medium height, with dark hair and eyes. She was a steady worker, quiet and kind, but there was a sense of sadness about her. Years later, her son, Abraham, seemed to have inherited her melancholy. By the time Nancy was nine, she had learned most of the arts and crafts so necessary for survival on the frontier. She then went to live with Richard and Rachel Berry as a hired girl. The Berrys were prosperous farmers in the Beech Fork area.

Kentucky, now with a population of more than 100,000, was admitted to the Union in 1792 as the fifteenth state and the first west of the Alleghenies. Lucy's father, Joseph Hanks, (Abe Lincoln's great-grandfather), died in 1793 and was buried in the Community Cemetery. General "Mad" Anthony Wayne made peace with the Indians in 1795, ending an era of hostilities.

Boone's land troubles continued to haunt him. He and Becky moved back to Kentucky near Brushy Fork, seven miles south of lower

28. Restored cabin of Daniel Boone's last home in Kentucky (1795-99), located on private property off U.S. Highway 68, seven miles south of the Blue Licks Battle Field where Daniel lost his son, Israel, in the last battle of the American Revolution, August 19, 1782. The logs in front of the cabin were cut by Daniel.

Blue Licks. During the four years they lived there, the state named a county in his honor, while two other counties seized ten thousand acres he owned.   With Kentucky now a full-fledged state, in 1796 the Wilderness Trail was widened to handle wagon traffic and renamed the Wilderness Road.

At age nineteen, Tom Lincoln served a short time in the Kentucky Militia. He was also a part-time jailer at Elizabethtown.

Lucy's younger sister, Nancy, for whom her daughter was named, had a love affair with Charles Friend. He had been a scout for General Washington. The result was another out-of-wedlock pregnancy in the Hanks family.   Nancy's son, Dennis, was born in Hardin County, Kentucky, in 1799. He lived with his Aunt Betsy and Tom Sparrow, who were childless. His cousin, Nancy, was living there at the same time. For several years, the four were never far apart.

Chapter 7
Missouri (1799)
Last Boone-Lincoln Migration

Tempting stories had reached Boone about Missouri, which Spain then owned. Acting as his grandfather did years earlier, he sent his son, Daniel Morgan, to Missouri to view and appraise the land and wild game. The governor heard about the elder Boone's interest and offered him a land grant of 8,500 acres and forty acres for each of his children who would accompany him to Missouri.

Boone cut down a large yellow poplar tree and built a canoe by hewing out the center. He then loaded part of his family and nearly all of his possessions into the canoe and started them down the Ohio River on an eight hundred-mile journey.

Boone and several other friends and relatives drove the cattle and horses overland to the small pioneer village of St. Louis. In early October, the family reached Cairo and then proceeded up the Mississippi to a rendezvous with the other group. A welcoming party met them and the Spanish governor, Zenon Trudeau, arranged a gala celebration. Boone was embarrassed by the lavish treatment, because never before had anyone celebrated any of his pioneer accomplishments.

The two groups consisted of Daniel, Squire and their families; Becky's relatives, the Bryans; Jemima's in-laws, the Calloways; and the Hannaniah Lincoln family.

Hannaniah Lincoln, not mentioned heretofore, was born in Exeter Township in 1756. He was the son of Thomas (grandson of Mordecai, Jr.) and his wife, Mary Robeson of Amity. Hannaniah was a captain in the Continental Army and fought in the battle of Brandywine. Soon after he left the army, he traveled to Boone's settlement in Kentucky where he bought 8,972 acres that Boone previously had surveyed for him.

Hannaniah and his wife, Sarah (Jeffreys) and their four children, Rebecca, Austin, Davis and Lucy joined Daniel in this final migration of the Lincoln and Boone families, thus ending a migration of the two families that began one-half century earlier. Tom Lincoln (Abe's father) had lived with Hannaniah and his family for a while in Elizabethtown before Tom was married.

The journey now continued up the Missouri River Valley for about sixty miles to the Femme Osage District near present Marthasville. Daniel, Becky and the family moved in with a son, Daniel Morgan, who had built a cabin on a bluff overlooking the river.

Incidentally, George Washington died the same year that Boone, now sixty-five, was starting life over on a new frontier. Colonel Boone was appointed the most powerful official in the district. He was a military and a civil officer, serving as sheriff, judge, jury and commandant. He held court under an elm tree which came to be known as the "Judgment Tree," and there he dispensed frontier justice.

He ignored all formal procedures and told all who came before him that he wished to know only the truth. Boone's most common punishment was the whipping post, where the lash was laid on well. He saw no need to send a man to prison when he was needed to till the land and provide meat for his family's table.

A good example of the kind of justice he dispensed was a case involving a poor widow and a landholder who were in dispute over a cow. It was clear that the man had the better case and Boone ruled in his favor. He then ordered the next defendant, a chronic disturber of the peace, to turn over one of his cows to the widow as his punishment.

Boone suffered much of his life from the courts, lawyers and judges, but now, in 1800, of all things, he found himself the chief maker of justice in the district. Long after his commission expired, people continued to go to the Judgment Tree for dignified justice and no record exists of an appeal from his decisions.

During the next few years, Napoleon coerced Spain into ceding back to France all of the Louisiana Territory including New Orleans, which was then a closed port to the United States. That caused a serious hardship for the western pioneers, because they did not have an open port from which to ship.

Later, when Napoleon found himself in a financial bind due to the wars in Europe, he sold the territory to the United States for $15 million during President Thomas Jefferson's administration. Although there was a question about the legality of the transaction, it was eventually completed, doubling the size of the Continental United

29. The "Judgment Tree," where Daniel Boone held court for three years under the auspices of the Spanish Government, located near Daniel Boones home in the Femme Ossage District, Louisiana Territory, near Defiance, Missouri.

30. School house in the Femme Ossage District, Louisiana Territory, located on Daniel Boone's property near Defiance,

States.   This meant that Boone had now been a citizen of four nations--Great Britain, Spain, France and the United States.

Tom Lincoln bought 238 acres on Mill Creek and built a log cabin there (now known as the Nall Farm).   It was located seven miles north of Elizabethtown in Hardin County, Kentucky.

Daniel Boone had four years of prosperity during which he accumulated several hundred acres.   However, in 1804, following the Louisiana Purchase, he once again found himself without any legal title to his land holdings.   He had failed to have them registered in his name.   His home was registered in his son Nathan's name in New Orleans.

To lose everything again at age seventy was most discouraging.   His sons and daughters had filed the necessary papers and they retained legal deeds to most of their property.

Squire, also having lost all of his property, moved to Harrison County, Indiana and built a home and gristmill near Corydon (the mill is still operating).   He died there in 1815 and was buried in a nearby cave known as Boone's Cave.

Daniel built his last cabin, a small one, on the property of his son, Daniel Morgan.   He and Becky were blessed by having five of their children--Susannah, Jemima, Daniel, Jesse, Nathan--and their families living nearby.

Meriwether Lewis, President Jefferson's private secretary, and William Clark, younger brother of George Rogers Clark of American Revolutionary and Indian wars fame, were selected by the president to form an expeditionary force to explore the newly acquired Louisiana Territory.

As they paddled their way up the Missouri from St. Louis, they stopped to seek Colonel Boone's counsel because of his expertise in dealing with the Indians and his advice on exploring a vast, unknown land.   Boone's was the last white man's cabin Lewis and Clark encountered before they entered the unexplored territory.

Since Boone personally knew President Jefferson and William Clark's brother, George, those two men could have been instrumental in having Lewis and Clark visit him in Missouri before their great venture into the wilderness.   Lieutenant Zebulon Pike, who was

31. *Reconstructed home built by Thomas Lincoln (father of President Lincoln), in 1803, along Mill Creek--located six miles north of Elizabethtown, Kentucky, in Hardin County. Tom and Nancy were said to have lived here for a short time in 1808. It is now part of*

credited with discovering Pikes Peak, also sought Boone's advice at about the same time.

In 1805, Tom Lincoln was hired to take a flatboat, loaded with bacon and other farm produce, down the Ohio and Mississippi rivers to New Orleans.

On June 12, 1806, Tom, twenty-eight, and Nancy Hanks, twenty-two, married in a small log chapel near the Richard and Rachel Berry home in Beechland on Beech Fork, Washington County.

Tom and Nancy's paths had crossed for the first time twenty-one years earlier as Boone escorted their families through the Cumberland Gap, but they would have been too young to remember the event. They courted for several months before the Reverend Jesse Head of the Methodist Episcopal Church officiated at their wedding. It is quite likely that Tom and Betsy Sparrow and Nancy's mother, Lucy, and her husband, Henry, and Tom's mother, Bathsheba, and her other two sons, Mordecai and Josiah, were there to participate in the celebration.

They had barbecued sheep, bear meat, venison, wild turkey, duck eggs and maple lumps. A jug of whiskey was passed around for those who wanted something stronger than tea. More than likely, the festivities lasted well into the night, because the Virginia reel was in vogue at that time.

The bride and groom spent the night in the loft of the Berry home, although Richard and Rachel had died two years earlier. The next day, they rode horseback to Elizabethtown where they set up housekeeping in a small cabin, with just the barest of necessities. Nancy read the Bible and the couple attended the Little Mount Baptist Church, where they became members.

On February 10, 1807, Sarah, their first child, was born in Elizabethtown. Since Tom was away from home a great deal of the time doing carpentry work, Nancy had to do all of the house chores alone. She kept the open fire going for cooking and heating, washed the dishes, scrubbed the floor and mended the clothes. That left precious little time for herself. For a short time, Tom moved the family to his Mill Creek farm.

32. *Richard and Rachel Berry's home along Beech Fork in Beechland, Washington County, Kentucky. Thomas Lincoln courted Nancy Hanks here. They were married June 12, 1806, in a nearby chapel by Rev. Jesse Head, a Methodist Episcopal Minister. This building*

Chapter 8
Last Days of The Pioneer--
Birth of The Prairie Lawyer

In December 1808, Tom bought a three hundred-acre farm near the south fork of Nolin Creek, known as Sinking Springs, just two and one-half miles from Hodgenville, in Hardin County (now La Rue County). There he built a crude cabin with logs he had cut from timber nearby. It had a dirt floor, stick clay chimney, one small window and a door that swung on leather hinges. He moved his family there and struggled constantly with nature just to eke out a bare subsistence. Few people settled there because the soil was so poor.

On February 12, 1809, our sixteenth president, Abraham Lincoln, was born there. He arrived about sunup Sunday morning on a bed made of poles cleated to a corner of the cabin and covered with cornshucks. A storm was brewing outside and the wind blew snow through the cracks between the logs and across the bearskin that covered Nancy and her new baby. Abraham was named for his grandfather, who had been killed by an Indian while he was working in his cornfield.

It is doubtful that anyone except her husband was there to assist in the birthing, but later that morning he walked two miles to where Tom and Betsy Sparrow lived. Dennis Hanks, their adopted son, met him at the door and, upon learning of Nancy's baby, took off down the road to see the new family member.

Betsy arrived soon afterward and proceeded to wash and clothe the baby with a petticoat and a linsey shirt. She cooked dried berries with wild honey for Nancy, straightened things up a bit and kissed the new mother good-bye. Before leaving, she said, "I'll come again in the morning."

Dennis stayed overnight. He rolled up in a bearskin and slept on the warm hearth in front of the open fireplace. The next morning, Dennis held his new cousin for the first time. When the baby started to cry, Dennis handed him back to his mother. "Take him! He'll never 'mount to much," he said.

33. *Abraham Lincoln's birthplace - Cartoon*

34. *Historically accepted birthplace of our sixteenth President, Abraham Lincoln, located at Sinking Springs, along Nolin Creek, two and one half miles from Hodgenville, Kentucky in Hardin County (now La Rue). Thomas and his family lived here about two years. This log cabin with a packed dirt floor was reconstructed at this site in 1911.*

35. *Abraham Lincoln's birthplace cabin is enclosed within this marble shrine near Hodgenville, Kentucky. The fifty-six steps*

Throughout his youth, Abe Lincoln was doomed to hardships. His food was coarse and his clothing so scanty, they barely served the necessities of his existence.

Another of the many marriages between the Lincoln and Boone families took place when Hezekiah Lincoln (a great grandson of Mordecai, Jr.), born in 1764, married Elizabeth Boone (a granddaughter of Daniel's Uncle James).

Other events of interest included the marriage of Amos Lincoln (great great grandson of Samuel) to Deborah Revere (daughter of Paul Revere) in 1771. Deborah died in 1797 and Amos took her sister, Elizabeth, as his second wife. In the same year, his cousin, Jedediah, married Mary Revere, who was a sister of Deborah and Elizabeth. George Rogers Clark suffered a paralytic stroke and moved to his sister Lucy's house in Louisville where he died in 1818.

After a couple of years at Sinking Springs, Tom Lincoln bought a farm about ten miles to the east at Knob Creek and moved his family there in 1811. The soil was richer, but life for Tom and his family did not improve greatly. In that same struggle was a neighbor, Joseph Hanks, a cousin of Nancy's.

When a youngster, little Abe was a great help and comfort to his mother, doing small chores around the cabin such as cleaning out the fireplace, keeping the wood box filled and carrying the drinking and cooking water from the well. As he grew, he learned the feeling of a blister as he helped his father hoe in the cornfield.

In 1812, another baby, Thomas, was born. Neighbor ladies came and helped, but a few days later the little one died and was buried in a coffin his father had made. He was the last of Tom and Nancy's children.

Almost daily, Abe saw settlers in covered wagons going past the Knob Creek farm on the pike which ran from Louisville to Nashville. Peddlers occasionally went by with their tinware and notions and slave traders were seen riding their horses while herding their ill-clad, barefoot slaves along the dusty road.

When Abe was about seven, he and his sister, Sarah, attended what was known as a "blab school" where they learned the alphabet and their numbers from one to ten. Abe also learned to form letters and to write a little under the direction of his first teacher, Zachariah Riney.

36. *Knob Creek Cabin - Thomas and his family lived here from 1811-1816. Here young Abe and his older sister, Sarah,*

At that age, Abe's muscular power, because of hard work, grew much faster than his scholastic talents and his character began to mold in a way that was to stand him in good stead throughout life.

During the War of 1812, the British again incited the Indians to make life miserable for the frontier people. Boone and his family were forced to flee overland to a fort for their safety. His son-in-law, Flanders Calloway, loaded all of their personal belongings into a canoe and they started down the Missouri River. Shortly afterward, the canoe struck a rock, capsized and everything was lost. The most significant loss was Boone's personal diary which had a long period of time recorded in it and could not be replaced.

Boone was among the first to volunteer to fight in the war but was rejected because of his age. His sons and grandsons were in the proper age range and they enlisted. Most pioneers in the West thought it was a good idea to trounce the redcoats and their Indian allies again, thus opening up more land for settlement.

The Americans confidently thought they could conquer Canada, but the only notable thing that happened for their benefit was bringing into prominence men such as Henry Clay, John C. Calhoun, Daniel Webster and Andrew Jackson. These were the kind of men who shaped the national policies of the United States for a generation.

For Boone, who stood ready with his rifle but did not get to use it, this was a time in which he suffered a grief more painful than anything he had yet endured. It was maple-sugaring time in the spring of 1813 and he had taken Becky to Jemima's to help boil maple sap. Becky suddenly became ill and, within a week, she died on March 18. Six of their children had preceded her in death.

Becky had followed Daniel from her father's home to scenes of danger for which no parallel was to be found. She had mourned him as dead when he was captured by the Indians; had faithfully and lovingly brought up his sons and daughters to cherish and love him; had been by his side when the murderous blows of the savage had laid their first-born son in a bloody grave; and thus had fulfilled the love and affection of a dutiful and faithful wife.

Becky was seventy-six when she died and was buried in Bryan's Cemetery located on the summit of a ridge above Tugue Creek, one mile southeast of the present town of Marthasville. Boone had selected the site and designated the adjoining plot to be his grave. He then abandoned his lonely cabin and spent most of his time with his children.

Within a year of Becky's death, the United States Congress passed a bill granting Boone 850 acres in recognition of services rendered. He could not have cared less, because he did not have Becky to share it with him.

When the people he still owed in Kentucky heard about the grant, they rushed to Missouri to demand payment and Boone sold his newly acquired land to pay off some of the old debts. He once again found himself without any land, but he no longer cared; he was old and his children had enough property of their own.

Boone had passed his eightieth birthday when he set out by canoe to explore the Platte River, following it to its source in the Rocky Mountains. He then traveled overland by foot to Yellowstone where he spent the entire winter trapping. The steaming geysers, bubbling mud pots and mountains taller than any he had ever seen, were like a fantasy world to him.

After traveling more than eight hundred miles in wilderness territory, Boone returned home in 1815 with his final cache of fur pelts and with one desire before he died. That desire was to return to Kentucky for one last time and pay off his remaining debts.

He sold the furs and took a flatboat down the Missouri River to the Mississippi and up the Ohio to Corydon, Indiana. He visited his brother, Squire, who had settled there after returning from Missouri. Daniel then went on to Maysville, Kentucky, where he visited his old friend, Simon Kenton, who had saved his life at Boonesborough many years earlier.

They were happy to see each other and talked for hours about their good and bad times. They had wanted to have a home in Kentucky more than anything else in the world. Both were denied that after settling it, defending it and making it safe for civilization. In parting, neither had a dry eye, because they knew they would never see each other again. Simon died in 1836.

Boone then proceeded to locate all who said he owed them, paying without question the amount each claimed. After all of his debts were paid, he gave a sigh of relief as he looked at the lone fifty-cent piece he had left, knowing he now could die an honest man.

37. *The only known portrait of Daniel Boone--painted by Chester Harding on an oilcloth in 1819. Daniel was 85 years old.*

Upon returning home in 1818, Boone spent his remaining days sitting on the bank of the Missouri, playing with his grandchildren. He watched the canoes and flatboats pass by as the new pioneers headed farther west to establish new frontiers.

It distressed him to know there would be no more long hunts. But in his reminiscing, he came to understand why he had not been able to build a fortune. He had never really cared enough about it.

He recalled how he had participated with General Braddock and Colonel Washington in the battle at Fort Duquesne during the French and Indian War; fought alongside his close friend and associate, General George Rogers Clark, during the American Revolution; and served in the Virginia Legislature with Patrick Henry and associated with Governor Thomas Jefferson. Now that the wintertime of his life had arrived, he sincerely hoped his fellow man would realize he had done his best.

One beautiful fall day on September 26, 1820, Daniel developed a fever while at Jemima's house but decided to ride over to visit his son, Major Nathan Boone, and have supper with his family. After eating a large portion of sweet potatoes, his favorite food, he became ill and that night, at the age of eighty-six, he died quietly.

A coffin that Daniel had made was pulled from beneath his bed and he was laid to rest beside Becky's grave. Now they were together again. On September 9, 1845, the remains of Daniel and Becky were claimed by the Commonwealth of Kentucky and they were reinterred with military honors in a cemetery in Frankfort. There is now some question about whose remains were taken to Frankfort.

In a letter Daniel had written to Sarah Day Boone, his brother Samuel's wife, he gave an insight into his religious beliefs:

"All the religion I have is to love and fear God, believe in Jesus Christ, do all the good to my neighbors and myself that I can and do as little harm as I can help and trust in God's mercy for the rest."

Daniel C. Beard (1850-1941) born in Cincinnati, Ohio, was a naturalist and author of books on camp lore, woodcraft and outdoor life. He immortalized Daniel when he organized the Sons of Daniel Boone, a forerunner of the Boy Scouts of America.

The Daniel Boone saga would now seem to be closing with the final chapter written by his death--but perhaps not. It would live on through

38. Daniel and his son, Nathan Boone, home. Built of limestone and the finest home in the Louisiana Territory at the time--located near Defiance, Missouri, approximately 60 miles up the Missouri River from St. Louis. It took seven years to complete. Daniel Boone died here September 26, 1820, at age 86, while visiting his son.

39. *Daniel and Rebecca Boone's grave site. Daniel chose this site overlooking the Missouri River Valley, near Marthasville,*

eternity in the hearts and minds of people of all ages, with hundreds visiting the grave site each year.

Chapter 9
Indiana (1816)
Lincolns Leave Kentucky--
Settle on Little Pigeon Creek

As it was with Daniel Boone and his loss of property in Kentucky, misfortune came to Tom Lincoln who also had failed to establish an adequate land title. Tom lost his Knob Creek farm to Thomas Middleton, who had secured a deed to nine properties in the area.

To the north of the Ohio River, across from Kentucky, was the Indiana Territory which was soon to become a state. Tom had heard from Austin Lincoln, son of Hannaniah, who had migrated to Missouri with Boone, about how fertile the land was and that it could be had for two dollars an acre, including a valid government deed. It was a place he could establish a home with confidence.

In 1816, Tom built a flatboat, loaded it with tools and household articles, said good-bye to Nancy and the children and headed for Indiana. While navigating one of the rivers, his boat capsized. He lost most of the household goods but managed to save his tools.

After reaching Indiana and spending time searching for the right spot, Tom finally selected and staked out an eighty-acre tract in Spencer County. The land was located about two miles from the small town of Gentryville and eighteen miles north of the Ohio River. He secured a legal title to this land on October 18, 1817.

When he returned home, Nancy had almost finished packing. They loaded the flat-bottom wagon, hitched it to the farm horse and started for Indiana. Nancy and Sarah rode in the wagon, Tom led the way, and Abe brought up the rear with the cow and family dog.

They left Knob Creek with everything they owned, leaving behind a few friends and relatives and a tiny grave in the churchyard. They were also leaving a state that condoned slavery, which Tom thoroughly disliked and were migrating to a free territory.

It was in Kentucky where they had found each other and it was the birthplace of their children. They had worked very hard but had few material things to show for their labors.

On their way north, they passed through Hodgenville and on to Mill Creek near Elizabethtown where they stayed overnight with Tom's sister, Nancy and her husband, William Brumfield. Tom visited with his mother, Bathsheba, who was living there at the time.

Bathsheba died in 1833 and was buried in the Mill Creek Cemetery which is now within the Fort Knox military reservation. In 1901, a slab of marble taken from her grandson's monument in Springfield, Illinois, was placed at her grave site.

Tom and his family slowly hacked their way through the wilderness and finally reached the Ohio River. They boarded a ferry which took them to the Indiana side landing at Anderson Creek near the small river village of Troy. It took two more grueling days before they reached their new home site, having traveled a total of about ninety miles.

The first snow of winter was falling when they arrived and Tom had little time to cut timber to build a cabin. A three-faced lean-to was hurriedly erected to provide some shelter for the family. It had no floor, door or window. It consisted of three sides and a slanting roof made of poles and brush to help keep out rain and snow. A fire at the open end was kept burning day and night for warmth and cooking.

Nancy and her two children slept there that winter, huddled together in a corner of the shed on a heap of leaves covered with bearskins. It was impossible to keep out all of the rain and snow. Nancy protected her children, especially at night, from the ever-present bears and screaming panthers roaming the woods in search of food. The poorly constructed lean-to was not adequate for human occupancy. A more concerned husband and father would not have expected his family to endure such hardships.

Food was scarce that winter because the growing season had passed when they arrived. They were forced to subsist mostly on deer and bear meat and an occasional duck, supplemented with nuts gathered from the forest. Tom occasionally would locate a bee tree. It was a tricky matter to smoke out the bees without getting stung severely, but it was worth all the effort because the raw honey was a delicious treat for the family. He tried raising hogs that winter, but bears kept eating them alive.

Tom and Abe worked through the hard winter building a log cabin near Little Pigeon Creek. Even though Abe had just turned seven, he

40. *A heavy snow was falling as Tom hurriedly constructed a three-faced lean-to which was to be their home for a cold winter. The mother and her two children slept together for warmth on a bed of leaves on a dirt floor. A more concerned husband and father would not have expected his family to endure such hardship.*

41. *Thomas Lincoln's reconstructed log cabin home from 1816 to 1830, located south of Little Pigeon Creek in Spencer County, Indiana, two miles from Gentryville and eighteen miles north of the Ohio River.*

was a great help to his father because he was large for his age. He felled some of the smaller trees, helped to cut and notch the ends of the logs and did most of the chinking, using wet clay and dried grass.

The cabin was completed just in time, in early spring of 1817, because Tom and Betsy Sparrow had arrived from Kentucky and planned to occupy the three-faced camp while their own cabin was being built.   Dennis Hanks, Aunt Nancy (Lucy's sister) and her husband, Levi Hall, were with the Sparrows. Most of the immediate family was now together again.

Sarah and Abe were growing tall and strong and, as most frontier children, were pressed into hard physical labor early in life. There was much to be done on the Pigeon Creek farm and they met the challenge well. Only the strongest could endure and pioneer men and women grew old at an early age.

Sarah was learning to cook, sew and do many other things a pioneer woman needed to know. Abe helped his father in the fields and learned the art of splitting logs into rails for fences. He seemed to thrive on deprivation and derived enjoyment from his severe lot.

The children went barefoot from late spring until the autumn frost when it became difficult, without shoes, to walk nearly a mile through the woods each day to fetch water from the spring and to walk to school and back.

Abe had less then one year of schooling throughout his youth. There was nothing in the area at the time to excite any ambition for education. He was eager early in life to learn and his cousin, Dennis, was very helpful at the outset of his book-learning. Abe spent hours at the fireside reading by the light of the burning logs, pine knots or even hog fat.

Abe owned no books and would walk miles to borrow one from a friend or an acquaintance.   One such book, *Weem's Life of Washington,* was owned by Andrew Crawford, a schoolteacher. A bit of misfortune befell that precious volume.   One night, after he had finished reading, Abe placed the book in a chink between the cabin's logs. Rain fell later on that night and the book was soaked.

Abe contacted the owner the next day with a woeful apology and then worked out an agreement whereby he would labor three days in Crawford's cornfield to pay for the damage to the book.

In the fall of 1818, Tom and Betsy Sparrow, Nancy's beloved foster parents, came down with milk sickness. It began with a whitish coating on the tongue and was caused by drinking milk from cows that had eaten white snake root. Tom and Betsy died in September and were buried in a little graveyard on top of a knoll not far from their cabin.

Abe's mother had spent many hours day and night nursing and caring for her dearest friends. Soon after their deaths, she fell ill with the same malady. She was burning up with fever, her pulse slowed and her hands and feet grew cold. Knowing she was dying, she called her children to her bedside and weakly spoke her last words to them.

They knelt beside her bed as she pleaded with them to be good to each other, to live as she had taught them and to worship God. Sarah and Abe suffered in silence, tears trickling down their cheeks. Nancy died quietly on October 5, 1818, at the age of thirty-five. It was the greatest type of loss any child could suffer on the frontier.

Tom and Dennis whipsawed planks from a log that was to have been used for the cabin floor and made a coffin for Nancy. The next day, the family carried the casket to the little knoll at the top of the hill and buried her in silence beside Tom and Betsy Sparrow and Levi and Nancy Hall. There was not a preacher in the area to give her a Christian burial.

Dennis Hanks, who had lived in the same home with Nancy for fifteen years, described her as having dark hair and a slender build.

Early the next spring, Abe wrote to Elder Elkins, who had lived near them in Kentucky, appealing to him to come and perform a delayed funeral service over his mother's grave. The good man cheerfully complied with the request and rode horseback about two hundred miles round-trip. Abe's kindness, humor, love of humanity and hatred of slavery all seemed to have come from his mother and her great Christian love influenced the development of his character.

Years later, Abe said, "All that I am or hope to be, I owe to my angel mother."

The vacant place of a wife and mother was sorrowfully felt in the Lincoln home. For several months, Tom spent most of his time in the woods hunting, leaving his motherless children and their cousin, Dennis, who was still living with them, to fend for themselves.

NANCY HANKS
LINCOLN
Mother of President
LINCOLN
DIED,
Oct. 5. A.D. 1818
Aged 35 years.

Erected by a Friend of her boundless Son

42 *Nancy Hanks Lincoln died of "milk sickness." This grave marker was erected after the assassination of her son, located*

Sarah cried and cried as she tried so hard to do the cooking, but nothing ever tasted right. The other chores were just too much for her. Most of all, there was no loving mother's hand or voice to guide her. Abe managed to keep the fire going and carried water from the spring.

They had no knives, forks or any soap with which to wash, so they ate what food there was with their grubby fingers. During the long winter months, they made no attempt to wash their bodies or tattered clothes and the bed of leaves grew filthy with fleas and other vermin. There was no sunlight to warm and purify the air in the dark, foul-smelling cabin and they grew more ragged and haggard daily. Abe endured more poverty in a few years in Indiana than thousands of the slaves he would one day liberate.

After living a year in such conditions, Tom could tolerate it no longer. He went to the creek one day, washed up a bit using sand and then headed for Kentucky, once again leaving Sarah, Abe and Dennis to shift for themselves.

Tom reached Elizabethtown within a few days and went straight to the home of Sarah Bush Johnston, whose husband had died three years earlier. Tom and Sarah had known each other from childhood. Sarah had been left with three children--Sarah, thirteen, Matilda, ten and John, nine--so Tom proposed merging their two broken households into one family. Sarah accepted Tom's proposal and they were married within a few days. After paying off Sarah's few debts, they loaded her household goods into a wagon and left for Indiana.

When they arrived at the Lincoln homestead, Sarah was appalled at the conditions she found in and around the cabin. She refused to unload her furniture from the wagon until Tom had installed a wooden floor in the cabin. In the meantime, she busied herself fixing and cleaning everything. She also bathed her new stepchildren, who looked so bedraggled.

The children were overjoyed to see a feather mattress, pillows, dishes, knives, forks and spoons, along with pots, skillets and a table and chairs. But most of all, young Sarah and Abe were delighted with their new stepmother. Warm and friendly, she immediately took charge of the desperate situation. She was to give them a new lease on life.

They now had three new playmates. With eight persons living together in a small, one-room cabin, it was very crowded. At bedtime, the men and boys would undress first, followed by Sarah and the girls and no one seemed ashamed or embarrassed.

Their new mother brought a certain joy into the home. She seemed to be the answer to a prayer, possibly that of Nancy's as she was dying. In her later years, Abe's stepmother always spoke of him with tender feelings.

"Abe never gave me a cross word or look and never refused anything I requested of him."

She was a rich, strong, silent force in his life, always guiding him and giving encouragement. She kept everything neat and clean and her faith in God showed in her actions more than her words. She also understood Abe's gloomy spells better than anyone.

The family lived together in harmony. The mother showed no partiality in her treatment of any of the children. Though Abe never forgot his "angel mother," he rewarded his new mother with a profound and lasting affection and devoted care. She proved a faithful friend and helper during the remainder of his childhood.

The Missouri Compromise bill was passed in 1820. It was to have a great effect on Abe's life in the future. It had to do with the proposed new State of Missouri being formed out of a territory and whether it should be a free or slave state.

Dennis related some years later that Abe was always a sensitive lad, never intruding where he was not wanted. He always lifted his hat and bowed when making his entrance and he was tender and kind, as was his sister.

Abe's stepsister, Sarah Elizabeth Johnston, fifteen, and Dennis Hanks, twenty-two, were married on June 14, 1821. Dennis and Sarah continued to live in the Lincoln household. They found a small place of their own when both families moved to Illinois a few years later.

When the folks were gone to a church meeting and the children were left alone, at times Abe would preach while the others did the crying. Often he would join in the chorus of tears.

John Hanks, a cousin of Abe's mother, Nancy, came to live with the Lincoln family in 1823. Now nine persons lived in a one-room cabin and all had to be fed and clothed. It also made sleeping conditions even more crowded.

Abe wrote with a pen made from turkey buzzard feathers, using pokeberry ink. He often used charcoal or a burned stick to write on the fence, floor or walls. He was quite proficient at writing and he wrote letters for his family, friends and sometimes for other settlers.

Once when Abe was attending Andrew Crawford's school, a young girl who spelled "definite" with a "y" was threatened and frightened by the teacher. Abe, with an understanding look, caught the girl's attention and put one of his long fingers to his eye, enabling her to change the letter just in time to escape punishment.

Schoolmasters were paid with corn, ham, venison, animal skins and other produce.

Abe always was encouraged in his studies by his stepmother but not by his father, who said, "I done fine without any larnin' and anyway, Abe is needed to work in the fields."

Abe was so interested in learning, he would put a book inside his shirt and fill his pockets with corn dodgers when he went to the field to plow. When noon came, he would sit under a shade tree and read while he ate lunch.

Once when Abe and a friend, Kate Roby, were sitting on the bank dangling their bare feet in the creek, she spoke of the moon rising. He explained to her that it was the earth moving, not the moon and that the moon only seemed to rise. Kate was amazed by Abe's knowledge.

Word got around at harvest time that Abe was "takin' the stump." Workers flocked around him and listened to his speeches with infinite delight. His disapproving father often would break it up with a strong hand. Abe was dragged from the platform many times and hustled back to work in a none-too-gentle manner.

"My father taught me how to work but not how to like it," Abe once said.

A man on horseback would ride up occasionally and Abe would be the first one astride the fence, asking questions till his father gave him a whack alongside the head. Although Abe was never sassy or quarrelsome with his father, that rough treatment seemed to generate an estrangement that lasted throughout their lives.

Abe had a passion for books and read everything he could get his hands on, including old newspapers. He had an excellent memory and never seemed to forget anything he had read. Some of his first and most important books, besides the *Bible*, were *Arabian Nights, Aesop's Fables, Robinson Crusoe, Pilgrim's Progress, History of the United States*, Robert Burns' poems and the speeches of Henry Clay, a leader in the Whig Party. When Abe finished reading Clay's speeches, he was a Whig, heart and soul.

To him, the most important book was the Bible. As he grew older, there was hardly a day he did not read something from the scriptures and, later in life, most of his speeches and state papers referred to or were biblically oriented.

Abe never seemed to have time for rowdy frolics, never drank liquor or used tobacco and swear words were not in his vocabulary. In later life, he became more religious-minded and attended church regularly at times, although he never officially joined a church. While in his teens, the family would come home from a church meeting and Abe would step atop a box he had placed in the middle of the floor. Then he would repeat the entire sermon, almost word for word.

Abe's grandmother, Lucy Hanks Sparrow, died in 1825 at the age of sixty. She had lived a fruitful life and was an asset to the frontier village. The sad news reached the Lincoln home in Indiana several days after her burial.

Abe, wearing buckskin pants, moccasins and squirrel skin cap, often walked several miles to attend court so he could listen to lawyers plead their cases. He would do his early morning chores, walk seventeen miles to Boonville, the county seat and spend the entire day in court. He then walked back home in time to do his evening chores before midnight. Abe heard one of the foremost lawyers in the region, John A. Breckenridge, during one of his visits to observe the court proceedings.

Years afterward, President Lincoln was in his office at the White House when an elderly man stood before him and said, "Mr. President, you don't know me."

Mr. Lincoln eyed him for a moment and said, "Yes I do. You're John A. Breckenridge. I used to walk thirty-four miles a day to hear you plead law at Boonville and your speeches at the bar first inspired me with the determination to become a lawyer."

When Abe's sister, Sarah, was nineteen, she married Aaron Grigsby in 1826 and a year later died during childbirth. She was buried in the graveyard of the Little Pigeon Creek meeting house.

Abe blamed his sister's death on neglect by the Grigsby family and hard feelings prevailed between the two families after that. This was Abe's second great loss within ten years and no doubt added to his melancholia throughout his life.

By his eighteenth birthday in 1827, Abe had attained his full height of six feet, four inches and was strong enough to hold a double-bitted ax at the end of the handle and extend it straight out from his shoulder without a quiver. He had become an expert at mauling logs into rails for building fences.

When he was in the forest felling trees for a clearing, the trees toppled so rapidly it sounded as if there were three men at work instead of one. At times, Abe would hire out to a neighbor for board and room, clothes and a small daily wage.

Abe earned his first dollar by constructing a flat-bottomed boat which he used to ferry two men and their luggage out to a steamboat. The steamboat was anchored in the middle of the Ohio River near Anderson Creek because there was no dock in that area. When the job was finished, each man threw a silver dollar into the bottom of his boat. Abe was elated, because never before had he earned more than thirty-one cents in a day.

As Abe continued his ferrying, it angered a Kentucky ferryman, John Dill. Dill hauled Abe before a Kentucky justice of the peace, Samuel Pate, for running a ferry without a license. Abe pleaded and won his first case in court, as Squire Pate ruled in his favor.

"I took the passengers only to the middle of the river. Therefore I did not violate the Kentucky statute," he said.

At one time, Abe hired out to James Taylor, working on his farm for six dollars a month. His labors consisted of clearing stumps from the fields, splitting rails, building fences, plowing fields and grinding corn on the hand mill. At hog-killing time, he helped wield the club, souse the dead swine in a barrel of scalding water, scrape the bristles and dress the meat. For that, he was paid an extra thirty-one cents a day.

In March 1828, Abe was hired out to James Gentry, the founder of Gentryville, to build a large flatboat for transporting a cargo of bacon and other farm produce down the Mississippi to New Orleans. He was assisted by his employer's son, Allen. Abe never before had been away from home or handled a business transaction of such magnitude, but his tact, honesty and ability saw him through with great success.

During the eighteen-hundred-mile journey, they were tied up to an embankment one night when seven Negroes attacked the future liberator of their race. Abe did well defending himself and his cargo. A few days later, they arrived safely at their destination where Abe saw an ocean-going ship for the first time and a city of 40,000 people. He also saw slaves in chains being herded through the streets to the slave market where they would be sold. Then and there, he learned to detest the institution of slavery.

After selling all of their merchandise, they boarded a steamboat for the trip home. The entire voyage took three months and Abe was paid twenty-four dollars. According to custom, until he reached the age of majority, Abe would give his father whatever money he had earned.

A great breakthrough in transportation had been achieved in America. In 1829, the Baltimore and Ohio Railroad inaugurated its first commercial passenger and freight service with a fourteen-mile run between Baltimore and Ellicott Mills, Maryland.

Chapter 10
Illinois (1830)
Goosenest Prairie

A new outbreak of milk sickness brought another scare to the settlement. Tom's farm was not producing very well and letters from John Hanks, Abe's mother's cousin, who was now living in Illinois, told about rich land which was producing abundant crops. All of this made Tom restless again.

He was feeding the chickens one fall day when they all turned on their backs, legs extended upright to be "tied for moving." Tom laughed and decided if the chickens were ready, then it was time once again for his family to find a new home.

They spent the winter preparing for the move. They built a wooden prairie schooner which was to be pulled by a yoke of oxen. In the meantime, Tom had sold his farm to Charles Grigsby for $125 and finally, the day to move arrived on March 1, 1830.

The wagon was loaded and the women and children climbed aboard while the men walked alongside, herding the cattle and driving the oxen. Abe's last moments were spent at his mother's grave site, tears flowing freely down his cheeks as he slowly made his departure.

Tom's household had grown to fourteen during the past few years. It consisted of Tom and his son, Abe; Sarah Bush Johnston Lincoln and her son, John; Dennis Hanks and his wife, Sarah Elizabeth Johnston, and their four children, Sarah Jane, Nancy, Harriet and John; and Levi Hall and his wife, Matilda Johnston and their son, John.

Travel was slow because there were no public roads, bridges or guideposts. The ground froze each night and thawed during the day, making the mud thick and slippery. They often had to ford small streams and rivers, sometimes breaking through the ice as they crossed. Each night, they camped along the way, cooked supper, fed the animals, bedded down and made an early start the next morning.

Abe once waded waist deep into an ice-filled stream to rescue their small dog that had jumped into the water after it had been left behind on the far side of a creek. After traveling more than two hundred miles, they reached the north bank of the Sangamon River, about ten miles southwest of Decatur in Macon County, Illinois.

John Hanks had already cleared and surveyed a site and cut enough timber to build a one-room cabin which was soon finished. Abe and John then cleared fifteen acres, split rails to fence the land and planted corn.

Tom and his large family were not destined to remain long in Macon County. The blizzard of December 1830 caught them ill-prepared. They had little meat, corn or wood laid by and they suffered greatly that winter.

As the roads became passable and "the chickens were ready once again," the Lincoln family and their kin moved seventy-five miles southeast to Goosenest Prairie in Coles County, about fourteen miles south of Charleston. Tom had thought of going back to Indiana, where they had experienced better weather, but changed his mind upon reaching Coles County.

Abe, now twenty-one and having reached the age of majority, decided to go out on his own. In February 1831, Abe, along with John Hanks and John Johnston were hired by Denton Offutt to take a flatboat of cargo to New Orleans. Offutt, a big-time promoter and heavy drinker, was to have the boat built and ready to go upon their arrival. They were to meet him on the Sangamon River near the village of Springfield.

When they reached their destination, they found their employer at the Buckhorn Tavern, lush with liquor and promises but no flatboat. Offutt then offered to pay each of them twelve dollars a month to build the boat. The three set about cutting timbers and floating them downstream to a mill. The logs were sawed into boards and used to build an eighteen by eighty-foot cargo vessel.

It took four weeks from the time the first timber was cut until they had the boat loaded with barreled pork, corn and live hogs and were ready to shove off. Abe was standing on deck in his homespun jeans and jacket with the legs of his pants stuffed inside his rawhide boots. A well-worn black felt hat was pushed slightly to the back of his head. He handled the steering of the craft most of the time and also cooked for the crew.

On April 19, as they rounded a bend in the Sangamon River at New Salem, the boat became stuck on top of the Rutledge milldam.

43. *Reconstructed home of Thomas Lincoln, his first in Illinois, located on the north side of the Sangamon River, about ten miles south of Decatur, in Macon County. He resided here only one year.*

44. *Reconstructed home of Thomas and Sarah Lincoln, their last, located at Goosenest Prairie, in Coles County, Illinois,*

45. Mr. and Mrs. Richard Harris, of Mattoon, Illinois, reenact the parts of Thomas and Sarah Bush Johnston Lincoln. A neighbor, Mrs. Robin Dimond, was helping with the dinner, located near Goosenest Prairie, Illinois.

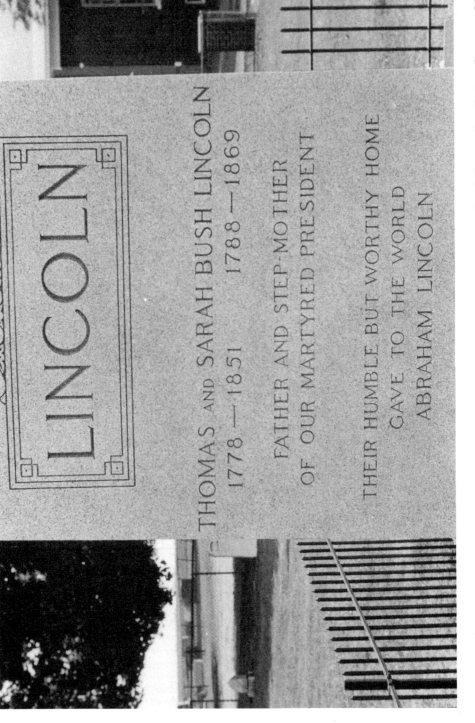

LINCOLN

THOMAS AND SARAH BUSH LINCOLN
1778 — 1851   1788 — 1869

FATHER AND STEP-MOTHER
OF OUR MARTYRED PRESIDENT

THEIR HUMBLE BUT WORTHY HOME
GAVE TO THE WORLD
ABRAHAM LINCOLN

46   Located in the Shiloh Cemetery, near the Lincoln Homestead, one mile north of Janesville, Coles County, Illinois.

It hung there for a day and a half while villagers gathered around. They were amused to see the tall lanky fellow solve the problem by unloading the cargo and boring a hole into the front of the boat so the water that had accumulated there would drain out.   As the craft became lighter, it smoothly lowered itself over the dam as the crowd cheered.   Abe plugged the hole, the men reloaded their cargo, and they headed downstream toward the Mississippi. The people in New Salem talked for days about how the long-shanked young man with a cool head and ready wit had solved the problem.

Abe furnished the amusement on the trip by telling his jokes and stories.   This brought lots of laughter and kept the crew in high spirits while doing chores.

Upon reaching New Orleans in May, Abe saw signs reading, "Highest cash prices paid for young Negro girls, ages ten through eighteen, also young healthy males." He saw Negroes in chains being whipped and maltreated as they were herded through the streets on their way to the slave market.

Abe recalled Thomas Jefferson's famous words in the Declaration of Independence: "We hold these truths to be self-evident, that all men are created equal, that they are endowed by their Creator with certain unalienable Rights, that among these are Life, Liberty and the pursuit of Happiness."

Abe thought, then why are these people being treated like animals? His heart ached for them and he was more determined than ever to hit hard at this injustice at his first opportunity.

The crew boarded a steamboat to St. Louis.   When they arrived, Abe walked overland to New Salem where the people had seemed so friendly.   Shortly afterwards, he was employed again by Offutt.   This time he was to manage a store and gristmill and be paid fifteen dollars a month, including a place to sleep in the back room of the store.

On August 1, 1831, Abe cast his first ballot, voting for Henry Clay who was running for Congress on the Whig Party ticket.   Abe made many new friends around the polls that day while enjoying his favorite pastime of joking and telling stories.

New Salem had become a thriving community of about one hundred people.   It served as a trading center for seven smaller communities within the area.   One of the communities, Clarys Grove, was home for a gang of ruffians.

Offutt was so impressed with Abe's physique that he boasted Abe would take on all comers in a show of strength. The Clarys Grove leader, Jack Armstrong, took up the challenge for a wrestling match. The day arrived and bets were placed.

The two contestants engaged in a frantic tussle for quite awhile before Abe pinned his opponent's shoulders to the ground. At that point, the wild, reckless, hard-drinking and hard-fighting Clarys Grove boys started to move in on Abe. He braced himself against a wall and was willing to take on anyone who wished to give it a try. Just then, Jack broke through the gang, shook Abe's hand and congratulated him on a fair contest. After that, they became very close friends.

In another instance, Abe was showing some yard goods to a couple of lady customers and a loudmouthed fellow interrupted, using foul language. Abe asked him to wait until he had finished with his customers, then he would be glad to oblige him in any way he wished.

The bully retorted, "No man can hinder me from saying anything at any time I want to."

As soon as the women were gone, the braggart began his verbal abuse again and Abe said, "Well, if you must be whipped, I suppose I may as well do it as anyone else."

Abe made short work of it by throwing him to the ground and rubbing his eyes with smartweed while the fellow bellowed with pain. Abe remained very calm about the situation and, knowing the man was in great misery, got a pan of water and washed the victim's face and eyes, alleviating some of his distress. Afterward, the man became a lifelong friend and was a better person for the experience.

Chapter 11
Lincoln Studies Law
Elected to State Legislature

There were three stores in the immediate neighborhood and it was evident that one was not going to make it. When there were no customers in the store, Abe used the time to study law books he had borrowed from a friend. Finally, Offutt's store petered out, leaving Abe without a job or money. However, he did have his strong hands and put them to good use doing odd jobs around the neighborhood.

Abe bought a horse and a set of surveyor's instruments on credit. He studied the art of the trade and did a bit of field work. At one point, he was not able to make a payment when it was due and there was a foreclosure on the equipment. A friend bought the instruments and the horse from the man who had foreclosed. He returned them to Abe, who was then able to continue his surveying.

Abe met Mentor Graham, the local schoolmaster, in 1832, who introduced him to mathematics and suggested that he study to improve his grammar. Abe became so involved that he joined the New Salem Debating Society, a group headed by James Rutledge, one of the village founders.

When spring came, Abe was encouraged to run for the State Legislature, which he did. His platform was short and simple: "Improvement of Navigation on the Sangamon River, Outlaw High Rates of Interest Being Charged by Lenders and Assure That Every Man be Given a Chance to Receive at Least a Moderate Education."

Once he was to make a speech in Pappsville, a neighboring community, and a large crowd had gathered. Abe looked somewhat odd wearing britches six inches too short, a checked woolen shirt, blue yarn socks and a straw hat without a band. As he began his speech, a loudmouth yelled, "Can't the party raise any better candidate than that?" and a fight broke out.

Abe calmly walked off the platform, seized the instigator of the tiff by the nape of the neck and seat of his pants and threw him out of the assemblage. He then returned to the stand and continued speaking.

He ended his speech by saying, "Fellow citizens, I presume you all know who I am--I am humble Abraham Lincoln. I have been solicited by my friends to become a candidate for the legislature. My politics are short and sweet, like the old woman's dance."

The man who earlier had started the fracas admitted later that Abe knew more than all of the other candidates put together. Since he was not very well known throughout the county, it was not surprising that Abe did not win.

About this time, the Indians decided the settlers were taking too much of their hunting grounds and turning them into farms. Chief Black Hawk, sixty-seven, of the Sac and Fox Tribes had allied with the British during the War of 1812 and now was leading the Ottawas, Chippewas, Winnebagos and Potawatomies on the warpath against the white man.

It was April 6 when the Indians started the destruction of the settlers' property by tearing down fences, destroying crops and slaughtering cattle. The red men ordered the people to leave their homes or face a massacre.

When the Black Hawk War broke out, Abe once again found himself without any means of support. According to him, he did not know much, so he enlisted for thirty days in the Fourth Illinois Volunteers.

When it came time to select a company leader, William Kirkpatrick and Abe were asked to compete for the position by having each volunteer stand behind his choice. Three-fourths of the men, including the boys from Clarys Grove, stood behind Abe the first time around. Finally, nearly all of them came over to his side. This was his first official honor and he was astounded at being selected captain by such an overwhelming majority. Years later he was heard to say, "Not since then has any success in life given me so much satisfaction."

Captain Lincoln then selected William Kirkpatrick, his rival, and Jack Armstrong as first sergeants of the platoons. Since Lincoln had no military experience up to this time, he had some difficulty with proper verbal commands. Once, when they approached a fence, he did not know the proper order to give so the men would go single file through the gate. He told the men to halt and break ranks for two minutes. Then he ordered the company to reassemble on the other side of the fence.

When Lincoln's first thirty days were up, and still without anything else to do, he reenlisted as a private in another contingent.   The mustering-in officer was Major Robert Anderson who, thirty years later, commanded, defended and finally surrendered Fort Sumter in South Carolina in the first conflict of the Civil War.

Lincoln saw no actual fighting but endured many hardships during that period.   The troops went without food for long periods while traveling on foot twenty or thirty miles a day through rough terrain. They also had to sleep on cold, damp ground, adding to their misery. He did shed some blood from time to time while battling the swarms of "man-eating" mosquitoes encountered on the way.   Hardships and deprivation were nothing new to Lincoln, so he fared fairly well.

He was mustered out of the volunteers shortly after the capture of Chief Black Hawk on July 21. His horse was stolen the previous night and he was forced to travel by foot and canoe more than three hundred miles back to New Salem. Six months later, he was paid ninety-five dollars for eighty days of service.

The villagers were anxious to hear about his war experiences. Among other things, he told them about the time an elderly, foot-sore and hungry Indian was found on the trail. The volunteers were ready to slay him, claiming he was a spy. However, Lincoln knew the old fellow was too feeble to be of any help to the warring Indians and ordered his release.

In that same war was Jefferson Davis, a young West Point graduate, who served as an officer in the Northern Illinois Army. About thirty years later, Davis was elected president of the Confederate States.

During the next few years, Lincoln worked at various jobs to keep body and soul together. He split rails, surveyed and became the postmaster for awhile in 1833, his first federal post. That gave him a chance to keep abreast of political news by reading the few newspapers that came through the mail. Lincoln was paid fifty dollars a year for managing the post office.

At one point, he and William Berry bought an old stock of goods on credit and opened a store. The venture was doomed to failure because Berry was an alcoholic. He drank up all the profits in a short time and soon died. Lincoln was left with his portion of the debts and he also assumed Berry's share. He later referred to this as his "national

47. *Reconstructed U.S. Post Office in New Salem, Illinois, where Abraham Lincoln was Postmaster in 1833. His first federal job.*

debt," and it took him more than sixteen years to pay off this obligation.

He was so destitute at times that he would live with the Jack Armstrong family. He was never idle while there, always helping with the farm chores. He also helped Jack's wife, Hannah, by cutting firewood, milking the cow or just rocking the baby's cradle, while at times he ate cornbread and drank buttermilk. In return, Hannah mended and patched his clothes. Lincoln always kept his law books handy and studied them whenever he could.

The hardships of poverty, absence of refinement and scanty formal education were surely of great value in building Lincoln's character--more than probably any heritage he might have received from his ancestors, with the possible exception of his unknown maternal grandfather. He chose to appear then, as in later life, precisely what he was--plain and humble.

Lincoln's personal qualities made him one of the most liked and trusted persons in Menard County. He was the best informed person in the region and acted as a judge, arbitrator or referee in many disputes, quarrels and games. He was strong and rough and yet the most gentle, kind and considerate man in the area.

Lincoln ran again for the State Legislature in 1834 as a Whig. While on the campaign tour, he pitched hay and cradled wheat in the field, showing the farmers he was one of them. He won that election by a large majority and was reelected in 1836, 1838 and 1840. He was elected again in 1854, but did not choose to serve.

When it came time for the Legislature to convene, he borrowed money to buy a "store-bought" suit, then walked more than one hundred miles to Vandalia, the capitol of Illinois. He was silent during most of his first term in the Legislature, observing and preparing for the future.

Once, when passing through Springfield from Vandalia, he bought a copy of one of Blackstone's law books at a sidewalk sale. Sir William Blackstone, an English jurist, wrote commentaries on the laws of England, the best-known treatise on English law and the foundation of legal training in England and the United States. That was a real find for Lincoln, because now he was earnestly pursuing the study of law to become a lawyer.

48. Grave site of Ann Rutledge, located in Concord Cemetery, near New Salem, Illinois. Abe and Ann were engaged to

During 1835 Lincoln suffered a despondent period due to the death of Ann Rutledge. She was the daughter of James Rutledge, the owner of the tavern where Lincoln was boarding. He loved Ann very much and they were engaged to be married, but they wanted to wait until he could earn his license to practice law and she could further her education.

Her death plunged him into deep despair. Lincoln was heard to say at Ann's grave site, "My heart lies buried there."

This was the third extreme tragedy to affect him mentally. The others were the early deaths of his mother and sister. It is believed that those memories cast a melancholy shadow over the remainder of his life, which he referred to as his "hypos."

After Ann's death, he lost all self-control and his grief seemed unbearable. Many of his close friends feared for his life, thinking he might be tempted to commit suicide. One very concerned family, Squire Bowling Green and his wife, Nancy, nursed him back to health during that period of deep depression. Lincoln became thin and looked haggard and careworn.

It was several weeks before he could resume any normal functions of life. He helped throw off his gloom and sorrow by leaping headlong back into the political arena.

Nearly thirty years later, Lincoln was heard to say, "I did honestly and truly love Ann and think of her often, even to this day."

Three important happenings took place in America at that time. One was the invention of the friction match. A fire now could be lit instantly and it was not necessary to keep a fire going at all times for cooking and heating. It previously was quite a chore to start a fire by friction or by flint and steel. The invention was received with enthusiasm as a great saver of time, fuel and discomfort.

Another significant but serious event came in 1836 when Davy Crockett from Tennessee, Jim Bowie from Georgia and Bill Travis from South Carolina banded together with 180 Texans to fight for liberty at the Alamo. Santa Anna, the leader of a Mexican army, stormed the improvised fortification, a small Franciscan monastery founded in 1718 and located in what is now San Antonio.

The small group of defenders withstood an onslaught of four thousand Mexican soldiers for eleven days. The enemy used cannons to destroy the walls surrounding the small complex and then they rushed through the gaps in the wall. In hand-to-hand fighting, the Mexicans killed all but three women and three children. The great American men who gave their lives made the supreme sacrifice for liberty.

Finally, a major breakthrough in long-distance communications took place that year when Samuel F. B. Morse invented the telegraph. Three years later, the first commercial line in the United States was installed between Washington and Baltimore. Previously, it took a whole day to get a message between the two cities, but it took only a minute or so with the telegraph.

In September, Lincoln passed the bar examination and was licensed to practice in Illinois. This fulfilled a great ambition he had been pursuing for a long time.

A great transformation took place in Lincoln's life during the six years he spent in New Salem. When he arrived, he knew only a couple of people in the community. Upon leaving, he had many friends throughout the whole area. He was an Illinois legislator, a practicing lawyer and was respected highly by those who knew him. Even so, he was still a young man without money and heavily in debt.

In the 1837 legislative session, Lincoln met Stephen A. Douglas in debate for the first time. This young man from Vermont had settled in Winchester, Scott County, Illinois, at the age of twenty-one. He first was a school teacher but later became interested in politics. It was in that session that Lincoln commenced his anti-slavery record which, incidentally, coincided with the outlawing of slavery in all British colonies.

Lincoln became the leader of his party in the House of Representatives and, as such, took an active part in the "Long Nine" made up of legislators and the main force that had the capitol of Illinois moved from Vandalia to Springfield.

Lincoln arrived in Springfield on April 15, 1837, riding a borrowed horse and with his entire belongings tucked in a pair of saddle bags. He reined in his horse at the general store owned by Joshua Speed, a man he knew slightly. He inquired about the price of a single bed with sheets, a blanket and a pillow.

When he learned the cost was seventeen dollars, Lincoln said, "That is perhaps cheap enough but, small as the sum is, I have not a cent and therefore am unable to pay. But, if you would extend me credit till Christmas and my experiment as a fledgling lawyer is a success, I will pay then. If I fail in this, I do not know that I can ever pay you."

Josh later said, "I never had seen so gloomy and melancholy a face or heard such a sad tone of voice." But realizing the financial difficulty Lincoln was in, he felt pity for him and offered to share his double bed with him.

Lincoln's face took on a different expression as he asked, "Where is your room?"

"Up there," Josh said, pointing to the stairs leading to the second floor.

Lincoln immediately went back to his horse, grabbed his saddlebags and rushed up the stairs two steps at a time. He soon returned and, beaming with pleasure, said, "Well, Speed, I'm moved in." He shared the room for four years and Josh soon became his most intimate friend, one he could take into his confidence.

In another stroke of good fortune, Lincoln was invited to take his meals at the table of William Butler, a friend he had made in the State Legislature, but there was no mention of board bills. However, when Lincoln became financially able, he paid a nominal fee for his meals and continued eating at the Butler home for more than five years.

On April 27, Major John T. Stuart and Lincoln formed a partnership. They had met during the Black Hawk War. Stuart was the leader of the Whig Party in Sangamon County and they had roomed together in Vandalia while serving in the State Legislature. Stuart had loaned him some law books and encouraged him to study for the legal profession. Lincoln, lacking any formal education, was self-taught and depended on his ability to think clearly and to express his thoughts forcefully but simply.

The capitol of Illinois was moved from Vandalia to Springfield, a thriving prairie community of around fourteen hundred inhabitants. It had wooden sidewalks, with an occasional pig running along the dirt streets. It also had horse-drawn carriages, four hotels, two newspapers, six churches and nineteen dry goods stores, drugstores and taverns. Eleven lawyers and eighteen doctors practiced there. Farm women were beginning to come to town wearing shoes instead of being barefoot and most of the men wore rawhide boots rather than moccasins. As for the townspeople, the more opulent men were starting to wear ruffled silk shirts and their wives dressed up in silks and laces.

Lincoln, now twenty-eight, was embarking on a new and different life-style. The first year of his law practice was a meager one. As he grew more confident in his presentations before the judge and jury and word got around about his courtroom victories, his services became more in demand.

At the July term of the Sangamon Circuit Court, Stuart and Lincoln represented sixty-six clients, compared to forty-five for Logan and Baker, their closest competitors. During their four years of partnership, the firm's average charge was five dollars a case. As Lincoln rose to a leadership level in the Illinois Whig Party circles, Stuart became a candidate for the U.S. Congress.

When Lincoln first began to ride the circuit, he was too poor to own his transportation, so he was compelled to borrow horses from friends. In due time, he purchased his own horse, Poky, which he fed and groomed. As time went on, he was able to buy a shabby one-horse buggy he called Rattlin. That was more comfortable than riding horseback, except during the rainy season when the rig often became mired in mud.

On December 9, 1839, the Illinois General Assembly met in its new capitol for the first time and a grand cotillion ball was held to celebrate the occasion. It was at this gala affair that Lincoln, the leading Whig member of the lower House, first met the girl he was to marry.

Mary Todd, twenty-one, from Lexington, Kentucky, had come to Springfield to visit her sister, Elizabeth, the wife of Ninian W. Edwards, Lincoln's colleague in the Legislature. Mary's grandfather, General Levi Todd, fought in the American Revolution, many times alongside General George Rogers Clark. Her father, Robert S. Todd, was a captain in the War of 1812, the president of a bank in Lexington and along with Henry Clay, was one of the national leaders in the Whig Party.

Mary was of average height, rather buxom and solidly built. She had a well-rounded face, dark brown hair and bluish-gray eyes. Her education was well above average, she was a good conversationalist and she wrote with wit and ability. Most of the time she was charming in her manner but, when offended or antagonized, her agreeable

49. Mary Todd Lincoln--Taken at the time she was the First Lady of the White House.

50. *Home of Mary Todd from 1832-39, located in Lexington, Kentucky.*

qualities quickly disappeared beneath a wave of stinging satire and sarcastic bitterness. Her tongue and her pen were equally sharp. In her physical proportions, education, social standing and temperament, she was the exact opposite of Lincoln.

Elizabeth Edwards was the focal point of Springfield's social life and was now ready to find a husband for Mary, next in line of the Todd sisters. There were about thirty eligible bachelors in Springfield at the time.

Lincoln approached Mary at the ball and said, "Miss Todd, I want to dance with you in the worst way."

As Mary remembered it, "He certainly did!"

That was the beginning of a courtship that was to have many ups and downs during the next several months. Mary's sister, Elizabeth, was not at all pleased with her selection of Lincoln from the other available young men. She argued that Mary was throwing herself away on a person who came from a different class of society. Ninian agreed with his wife.

At one point in 1840, it seemed as if they had decided to be married. However, Lincoln had second thoughts because of their many differences. Above all, he was concerned about how he could support a wife on his meager income when she was living on a much higher social level than he.

Lincoln told Mary one evening that he wanted to end their relationship. Mary was broken-hearted and she cried. They quarreled, made up and then quarreled again.

Was it jealousy on Lincoln's part? Mary did flirt with other men and, on occasions, was seen in the arms of Stephen Douglas at parties Lincoln did not attend. Or was it the incompatibility of their temperaments that brought things to a climax, causing them to part on New Year's Day, 1841?

Lincoln confided to Stuart, "I am now the most miserable man living."

He decided to visit his close friend Josh Speed, who had sold his store in Springfield in 1840 and returned with his mother to his farm near Louisville. Lincoln arrived in Kentucky in a depressed mental state. After a few weeks, with the help of Mrs. Speed, his melancholia lifted to an extent and he was able to return to his law practice in Springfield.

Lincoln's father sometimes found himself in financial difficulties. Once he bought three parcels of land but was unable to pay the contract. When the creditor threatened to foreclose, Lincoln came to his rescue, buying one tract for two hundred dollars and allowing his father and stepmother the use of it until the end of their days.

Lincoln's stepbrother, John D. Johnston, always seemed to be in dire straits. He wrote to Lincoln asking for eighty dollars. Lincoln wrote back suggesting that he go to work to cure his dire straits but did offer to give him one dollar for each dollar he earned.

Major Stuart, after being elected to Congress, dissolved their law partnership on April 14. Lincoln then formed a business association with Judge Stephen T. Logan, one of the most accomplished lawyers of that time. Under Logan's guidance, Lincoln became a formidable and resourceful prairie lawyer. In the December session of the Illinois Supreme Court, he argued fourteen cases and lost only four. In handling twenty-four cases in that court during the next two years, he won only fourteen.

As fall approached, Lincoln was invited to attend a party at the home of a friend, Mrs. Simon Francis, the wife of the editor of the Sangamon Journal. When he arrived, Lincoln was surprised to find Mary Todd among the guests. Mrs. Francis brought them together, saying, "Be friends again." From then on, they became steady companions.

In the meantime, Lincoln wrote to his friend, Josh, now happily married, asking his opinion about his renewed relationship with Mary. Josh advised him either to make up his mind and marry her or turn away from her entirely.

In the early morning of November 4, 1842, Lincoln went to call on his close friend, Judge James Matheny, to ask him to be his best man, explaining he and Mary were to be married that evening. That afternoon, Lincoln met Ninian Edwards on the street and informed him of the impending wedding and Ninian insisted the ceremony must take place at his mansion. That morning, Mary had asked Julia Jayne Trumbull to be her bridesmaid.

Ninian rushed home to ask Mary if what he had heard was true. She said, "It was decided last night and I didn't want to put it off for fear that a long engagement might not work out."

The parlor was made ready and the Reverend Charles Dresser was contacted. He performed the Episcopal ring ceremony that evening with only a few close friends attending. Lincoln had purchased a plain gold ring the day before. It bore an engraving, "Love is eternal."

Jim Matheny, when asked afterwards about the wedding, said, "Lincoln looked as if he were going to slaughter."

Within a few days, the Lincolns took up residence at the Globe Tavern. Mrs. Early was their landlady. Room and board cost them only four dollars a week.

From the outset, Lincoln found marriage "a field of battle, not a bed of roses." He met his domestic troubles with patience and avoidance as he suffered in silence. He became a pathetically sad and gloomy man and melancholia virtually dripped from him as he walked. There were times he would pass a friend on the street and not see him. On the other hand, if he recognized the friend, he was warm, friendly and most likely would tell a story or joke to cover his despondency. He preferred meeting friends away from home where he could be more at ease.

Their first son, Robert Todd Lincoln, was born August 1, 1843 and shortly afterward they bought a home on Eighth and Jackson streets from Reverend Dresser for fifteen hundred dollars. This was the only home Lincoln ever owned.

Bowling Green died in February and Lincoln went to the funeral at New Salem. His widow, Nancy, who had nursed Lincoln back to health during his illness following the death of Ann Rutledge asked him to speak at the burial site. He could not keep his composure and tears streamed down his face as he tried to express his grief. He managed to say only a few words.

Lincoln always did the family's daily marketing. With a basket on his arm and a small boy in tow, he would visit the butcher shop, vegetable stand and bakery. He found this time away from home very relaxing as he visited with friends. He continued to do the family marketing in Springfield, even after he was elected president.

51. *Abraham and Mary Todd Lincoln's residence on Eighth & Jackson streets in Springfield, Illinois. The only home Lincoln*

Lincoln was late for dinner quite often and this would create a scene that sometimes carried over till morning. He would then leave home shortly after his milking chores and pick up a piece of cheese and a few crackers at the market, eating them for breakfast while walking along the sidewalk. Upon reaching the office, he most likely went into a back room without speaking and remained there until he had regained his composure.

At the Whig convention in 1843, there were three well-qualified men vying for the seat in the U.S. Congress--Edward D. Baker, John J. Hardin and Abraham Lincoln. Lincoln worked out a plan whereby each would take a turn. The first two were elected and served their terms but; when it came Lincoln's turn, Hardin did not want to relinquish the seat. It took a few letters from Lincoln to remind Hardin of the previous agreement. Hardin, with great reluctance, finally withdrew from the race a few days before the election.

Lincoln's opponent, on the Democratic ticket, was Peter Cartwright, a well-known frontier evangelist circuit rider who once tried to embarrass Lincoln during a church service. Cartwright asked Lincoln whether he was going to heaven or hell.

Lincoln turned the tables on the evangelist by saying, "I'm going to Congress." Lincoln defeated his opponent 6,340 votes to 4,829.

During the campaign, Whig friends raised two hundred dollars for Lincoln's personal expenses. After the election, he handed back $199.25.

"I spent only seventy-five cents in the campaign and that was for a keg of cider I had bought for some of the boys," he explained.

In 1844, Lincoln's partnership with Logan was terminated and he took in William H. Herndon as a junior partner. Lincoln was now a full-fledged prairie lawyer, spending a great deal of time traveling the Eighth Judicial Circuit. He argued cases, pleaded, prosecuted and defended before the courts. Most lawyers on the circuit returned home each weekend or so, but Lincoln chose not to go home for months at a time.

Traveling the circuit was not all legal work. Lincoln used it to keep his political fences in order and to make new friends while preparing for the future. His law practice was his profession, but his passion was politics.

Life on the circuit was not an easy one. In the winter, the roads were covered with ice and snow. During the spring thaw, the mud was ankle-deep or deeper. At other times, there were no roads, just an unbroken prairie with streams to ford. Lawyers usually began their journey at dawn and traveled till nightfall in order to be at the county seat in time for court the next morning.

Court days were red-letter days and people from neighboring communities filled the courtrooms. They listened to the proceedings and were enthralled by the legal battles. Lawyers had little time to prepare their cases and reference books were not available. Frontier courts supplied not only justice but education and entertainment as well when sparring attorneys matched wits with able opponents.

Lincoln always tried a case as fairly and honestly as he could. He never intentionally misrepresented the testimony of a witness nor did he misstate the law in his own intelligent view of it. On the other hand, he could do little if he did not believe in the case.

Sometimes he would withdraw from a case when he found his client had deceived him. A judge once sent a messenger to request Lincoln to return to the court. He was found playing ball.

Lincoln said, "Tell the judge that I can't come--my hands are dirty and I came over to clean them."

Lincoln invariably held the attention of the jury, because he spoke the language of the people, using short, clear sentences. He took pains never to confuse the jury.

One of his clients was an elderly, crippled widow. He won the case, did not charge for his services and even paid her hotel bill. This was not unusual for him. His philosophy of law was, "If you cannot be an honest lawyer, then be honest without being a lawyer."

After a day's work in court, Judge Davis and the lawyers would gather around the hotel room, discussing philosophy, economics and politics. Lincoln was always the life of the party with his funny stories; his repertoire was inexhaustible. Periodically, he became immersed in dejection and nothing but elapsed time could change him. While on the circuit, he frequently studied subjects such as algebra, astronomy or even Euclid's geometry.

Judge Davis was more intimately associated with Lincoln than with any other lawyer on the circuit.   Often he sat in for the judge, instructed the jury and handed down the judicial decision.

In 1845, Lincoln was retained by the Illinois Central Railroad to represent it in a lawsuit.   He was successful in winning his case in the Supreme Court and billed his client five thousand dollars for his services.   The railroad refused to pay, claiming it could have gotten a first-class lawyer for that amount.

Lincoln sued the railroad and received a judgment in his favor.   The railroad still refused to send him his fee, so he put a lien on a parcel of property owned by the railroad.   That brought a check posthaste.

Lincoln was the only Whig candidate from Illinois to be elected a representative to the lower House of Congress that year.   He had a majority of 1,511 votes.   Even though his fight against slavery was not very successful at the time, he did manage to strike his first blow nationally.   He voted for the Wilmot Proviso which would have barred slavery from the territories acquired from Mexico.   The proviso did not pass, but it brought sharply into focus the question of the extension of slavery.

A second son, Edward Baker Lincoln, was born March 10, 1846. The joy of this child was not to be shared for long by the family.   He died four years later in February 1850.

Lincoln took his seat in Congress in December 1847.   Mary and the two children went with him to Washington and they lived at Mrs. Ann G. Sprigg's boarding house.   Mary was soon on her way back to her family home in Lexington.   Living in a boarding house in Washington was not conducive to the social life she had expected.

When Lincoln began his term, the war with Mexico was almost over and the Whigs, bowing to public pressure, were willing to accept the annexation of upper California, Texas, Utah, Nevada, Arizona, New Mexico and parts of Colorado and Wyoming.   The lower Rio Grande River became the boundary of Texas.   The United States agreed to pay Mexico $15 million for the territory acquired during the war and assumed about $3.25 million in Mexican debts to American citizens.

In President Polk's message to Congress, he reasserted that it was Mexico, not the United States, which had started the war.   He also said that Mexico had struck the first blow and had shed the blood of

52.   Lincoln's earliest known photograph (probably taken in Springfield, Illinois) at the age of thirty-seven. He was elected to the U.S. House of Representatives at the time.

Americans on American soil. The Whigs contended the president was not telling the truth.

Lincoln made three speeches during his first term. He also submitted an eight-point resolution in which he asked the president to inform the House if it was United States soil where the first blood of the war with Mexico was shed.

The people back home became angry with Lincoln. One newspaper called him a "second Benedict Arnold." He understandably did not win reelection. As the war progressed, he did vote for the bills to supply the soldiers with the necessities to carry on the fight.

After adjournment of Congress on August 14, 1848, Lincoln went to the New England states where he made various speeches on the issue of "Slavery Is an Evil." While in Worcester, Massachusetts, he was a dinner guest of ex-Governor Levi Lincoln, a distant cousin, though the family connection was unknown to either of them at the time.

Arriving back home, and probably thinking his political career was over, he found to his surprise he had been selected as a representative to the National Whig Convention. He also finally managed to pay off his "national debt," the obligation he had acquired in New Salem sixteen years earlier when his business partner died and Lincoln assumed the total indebtedness of both of them. He accomplished the payment despite an average yearly income of only fifteen hundred dollars and part of it was paid in the form of groceries and farm produce.

Lincoln never neglected his house chores when he was home. He still cut the firewood, tended the stoves, curried his horse, milked the cow, churned the butter and did the marketing.

He sought the position of U.S. General Land Office commissioner in 1849 but was unsuccessful. He later declined the office of governor of the Oregon Territory because Mary did not want to move there.

On March 7, 1850, Lincoln was admitted to practice law before the U.S. Supreme Court. He lost his first case.

William Wallace (Willie) Lincoln, a third son, was born December 21. Willie seemed to be his father's favorite. When Willie died twelve years later, while the Lincolns occupied the White House, his father found it one of the most trying times of his life. For several months he was unable to retain his composure when Willie's name was mentioned.

The Lincolns rented a pew in the First Presbyterian Church in Springfield where Mary took the sacraments and became a member. Lincoln did not join the church, saying, "I can't quite see it." He read the Bible though and knew it from cover to cover. He knew its famous texts, stories and psalms. He quoted it frequently in speeches, letters and talks to juries. Some thought his views were similar to those of the noted preachers of the day.

As the slavery issue grew larger in the minds of the people, it is interesting to note there were 405,500 mulattoes in the United States and nearly all came from black female slaves and their white masters.

Lincoln's father, Thomas, died January 17, 1851 and was buried in the Shiloh Cemetery, located about one mile north of Janesville in Coles County. His only son, Abraham, could not attend the funeral because of a crowded court calendar, including Supreme Court cases.

Lincoln concluded that a small crumb of affection is definitely more painful than pleasurable. However, his love for his stepmother was on a higher plane. He was grateful for her love and everything she had done for him. She also was very devoted to him, even more than to her own son, John, who had recently tried to get her to sell the farm and move to Missouri. Since Lincoln owned the farm, she would not consider such a foolish thing. For years Lincoln helped to support his aged father and stepmother and always visited them when he was nearby while on the circuit.

Lincoln had habits that were hopeless for Mary to try to break. For instance, he chose to lie on the front room carpet on his back while reading; came to the table without a coat; and ate with his eyes and thoughts focused elsewhere. She also tried desperately to get him to let the servant answer the front door, but Lincoln continued doing it, wearing carpet slippers and in shirt-sleeves.

A lady once knocked at the door and asked for Mrs. Lincoln. He said, "She's upstairs getting into her trottin' harness." That would have mortified Mary had she heard it.

Mary wanted to be a leader in society, so she constantly prodded her husband to keep up his struggle to improve his position, knowing it would elevate hers as well. All the while, her terrible temper and tongue never rested.

Herndon later wrote in a description of his partner, "Lincoln was the most secretive man I ever knew." A lawyer who tried cases with him said, "You can never tell what Lincoln is going to do until he does it." Lincoln not only proved himself equal to every task but gave, from the outset, the impression of possessing a great reserve of force.

The Lincolns' fourth son, Thomas (Tad), was born April 4, 1853, with a cleft palate which left him with a speech impediment, making it difficult for people to understand him. He was mischievous and able to get away with it.

Tad probably caused more excitement and commotion around the White House than any of its previous occupants. His father never closed the door to him, regardless of how important the meeting. Lincoln always had time for his children, walking with them perched on his shoulder or pulling them along the sidewalk in a wagon. This was also another of his ways to get out of the house.

Lincoln and Herndon paid little attention to bookkeeping, dividing the fees equally. Herndon was bothered frequently as his partner told the same story on the same day to one client or politician after another.

Herndon once wrote of Lincoln's physical makeup: "In walking, he put his whole foot down on the ground at once, not landing on the heel; he also lifted his foot all at once, not rising from the toe. He didn't wear clothes; they hung on him."

The enduring power of Lincoln's brain was tremendous. Herndon also said, "He could sit and think without food or rest longer than any man I ever met." Lincoln's hat was his office, where he tucked in little pieces of paper on which he had written his thoughts.

It perturbed Herndon when Willie and Tad came to the office with their father on Sunday morning while their mother was at church. The boys were totally unrestrained as they pulled books off the shelves, upset ink bottles, bent the pen points and threw them into the spittoon. Their father sat at his desk working as if the office were empty, while his unfortunate partner thought much but did nothing.

The records show that the Lincoln-Herndon partnership handled thirty percent of the Circuit Court cases in Sangamon County in 1854. Considering there were approximately twenty practicing attorneys in Springfield, the partners enjoyed the lion's share of the legal business.

From the time Lincoln's term ended in Washington in 1848, he was virtually in political retirement. It took a bombshell to launch him back into politics and it was triggered by passage of the Kansas-Nebraska Act by Congress on May 30, 1854. Lincoln was convinced the act was unjust and unwise.

Stephen A. Douglas was author of the act which, in effect, repealed the Missouri Compromise that allowed people in the territories to decide for themselves whether to allow slavery within their borders. This accelerated the chain of events which led directly to the conflict over slavery.

In a powerful speech at Peoria, Lincoln stated his reasons for opposing the spread of slavery. His reasoning and eloquence were so compelling that he was catapulted at once into fame as a leader among the champions of the anti-slavery cause.

The Whig Party had lost favor during the war with Mexico. Two years later, on May 29, 1856, at Bloomington Lincoln assisted in organizing the Illinois Republican Party and threw his whole support behind it. Its platform insisted that under no conditions should slavery be allowed to expand. Lincoln made more than fifty speeches during that time.   His name was presented to the National Republican Convention as a candidate for vice president, but he lost to the better-known party leaders in the East.

Lyman Trumbull's wife, Julia Jayne, had been a close friend of Mary's over the years, having served as bridesmaid at her wedding in 1842. While still single, they joined in writing verses and letters to the Sangamon Journal. But when Julia's husband won an election over Lincoln, Mary refused to speak to her ever again or to receive a call from her.

A lawyer was talking business with Lincoln at home one day when the kitchen door opened suddenly. Mrs. Lincoln poked her head in and snapped a question as to whether her husband had done an errand she had told him to do.

Lincoln looked up and quietly said, "I have been busy but will attend to it as soon as I can." Slamming the door, Mary wailed, "I am neglected, abused and insulted."

The visiting lawyer, wide-eyed, muttered his surprise. Lincoln laughed, saying, "Why, if you only knew how much good that eruption did for the little woman, you would be glad she had the opportunity to explode."

Judge David Davis once said, "Mr. Lincoln's honor saved many a woman. This I know. I have seen him tempted and I have seen him reject the approach of women on numerous occasions."

A man on the street one day asked Lincoln for advice on a point of law and he told the man, "I'll have to look it up."

When he met the man again, he gave him the advice he had wanted. The man wanted to know the fee and Lincoln answered, "There will be no fee, because it was a point I should have known without looking it up."

A client once insisted that Lincoln bring suit against a crack-brained lawyer for $2.50. Lincoln collected a $10 fee in advance, entered suit, gave the defendant $5 and asked him to show up in court and pay the $2.50 debt, which he did. Everyone was satisfied. It cost the claimant $10 to collect $2.50 and the defendant made $2.50 in the deal. Lincoln made $5.

In many cases, where a poor client had justice on his side, Lincoln charged no fee and sometimes quietly slipped the client five or ten dollars.

Lincoln once argued a case to a jury which brought in a verdict of guilty. After giving the case further consideration, he thought the man was truly innocent and spent several months working on the case until the governor pardoned the man. Over a period of twenty years, Lincoln signed twenty petitions for pardons of convicted men and the governors of Illinois granted fourteen pardons.

Dred Scott was a Negro slave who belonged to an officer in the U.S. Army stationed in Missouri, a slave state. His master had been ordered into a free northern state and territory in 1857. While there, Scott married a Negro woman and took her back to Missouri with him when his master was ordered to return.

After a time, his master died and Scott tried to gain his freedom through the courts. He claimed that he was free because he had lived in a free state where slavery was forbidden. The case finally reached the U.S. Supreme Court, where it was ruled that Scott was still a slave.

The court declared that a Negro could not be regarded as a citizen because he was a property. If a slave owner took his property into a territory where slavery did not exist, the law in that area could not take that property away from him. This meant that Congress had no power to prohibit slavery in the territories.

Supreme Court Justice Roger B. Taney, who handed down the decision, believed that the Constitution did not refer to Negroes when it spoke of "citizens" and, in the Declaration of Independence, "all men" excluded blacks as being inferior and unqualified to enjoy rights accorded to whites.

Senator Stephen Douglas defended the decision, but Lincoln asked, "Then why did they insert in Article I, Section 9 of the Constitution a provision prohibiting the slave trade after 1808?" A few years later, Scott and his wife were freed by their subsequent owner.

It was early in May 1858 when Lincoln traveled to Beardstown to defend Duff Armstrong on a charge of murder. Duff was the son of his dear friends, Jack and Hannah. He was accused of killing James Metzker on a moonlit night on August 29, 1857.

One witness, Charles Allen, swore that he saw Duff hit Metzker with a slingshot at 11 o'clock that night. Lincoln asked the sheriff for an almanac and used it to prove the moon was not bright at that hour but was setting. Therefore, Allen would have been unable to see the incident as he had testified.

During his statement to the jury, Lincoln pointed to Duff's tearful mother, Hannah, and recalled how she had washed and mended his dirty clothes and had given him food and shelter when he had no money to pay. How could a son of such a kindly woman be a murderer? Hannah, overcome with emotion when the jury returned a verdict of not guilty, grabbed Lincoln's hand. He made no charge for his services and gave Hannah money for train fare back home.

Chapter 12
Lincoln - Douglas Debates

In June 1858, Lincoln was nominated for the U.S. Senate from the State of Illinois at the first convention of the newly formed Republican Party. His opponent, on the Democratic ticket, was Stephen A. Douglas, who was called "The Little Giant" because of his massive head and shoulders and short stature. He was barely five feet tall.

Douglas was a formidable debater, orator, resourceful political leader and one of the greatest public figures of the day. As a U. S. Senator from Illinois, he was now considered the head of the Democratic Party in the North and South.

The Democrats claimed the only way Lincoln could draw a crowd was to take advantage of the audiences the more prominent Senator Douglas attracted. Each attended the other's meetings in order to reply at a later time to his opponent's charges.

To simplify things, Lincoln challenged Douglas to a debate. After some deliberation, Douglas took up the challenge and it was agreed that there would be debates in seven towns around the state.

Lincoln gave his speech, "A House Divided Against Itself Cannot Stand," saying, "I believe this government cannot endure permanently half slave and half free. I do not expect the Union to dissolve--I do not expect the house to fall--but I do expect that it will cease to be divided. It will become all one or all the other."

Douglas, as an attorney for the Illinois Central Railroad, had a special train which transported him in comfort and style from place to place. Lincoln made his way as best he could. Once he was riding on a freight train which had to be switched to a siding for several hours in the hot sun just to let Douglas's train pass.

At their second meeting, which was at Freeport, Lincoln prepared a trap for Douglas which changed the course of American history. Lincoln asked Douglas if the people of a territory could exclude slavery. According to Douglas's doctrine of popular sovereignty, the answer should be yes, but according to the Dred Scott decision, which declared that Congress had no power to exclude slavery from a territory, the answer would be no. If Douglas answered yes, he would displease the South. If he answered no, he would lose the support of the North.

53. The Statehouse in Springfield, Illinois, where Abraham Lincoln delivered the "House Divided" speech and later set up

Douglas answered, as Lincoln had expected, that "no matter what the courts might do, slavery cannot exist a day or an hour unless it is supported by local police regulation and that a territory could, by unfriendly legislation, keep out slavery."

The immediate results of the debates were a great disappointment to Lincoln, who declared, "I am like the boy who stubbed his toe. It hurt too bad to laugh and I was too big to cry."

Lincoln's popular vote was four thousand more than Douglas's, but he still lost the election. Douglas, the incumbent, had control of the state political machine and through it had gerrymandered the State Legislature into giving him fifty-four votes to Lincoln's forty-six. Even though Lincoln lost the election, he was now a figure of national importance because the debates brought him recognition and prestige he had not known before.

Financially, the 1858 campaign was a disaster for Lincoln. During that time, he had dropped his law practice and had no income. He did manage to pay travel and lodging expenses from his small savings. He arrived home at the end of the campaign without any money, not even for household expenses.

Chapter 13
Campaign--Elected President

In 1859 a fellow Republican, Jesse Fell, a land trader and railroad promoter from Pennsylvania, told Lincoln that he was being considered in the East for the presidency.

Fell said, "We need a man of popular origin, of acknowledged ability and committed against slavery aggression, who has no record to defend and is of good character."

Lincoln later wrote to one newspaper editor, "I must in all candor say I do not think myself fit for the presidency." As time passed and he became more involved in national affairs, Lincoln changed his mind.

Now that Lincoln had become a national figure, he was being bombarded with requests for speaking engagements all over the northern part of the country.

Early in 1860, he accepted many of them, including one at the Cooper Union Institute in New York City where he delivered one of his most famous speeches.

It was February 27 when Lincoln viewed the largest audience (fifteen hundred) to be assembled since the Clay-Webster days. Horace Greeley, one of the founders of the Republican Party, sat beside him on the platform. William Cullen Bryant, "Father of American Poets," made the introduction.

Most of the people present had never watched Lincoln walk, noticed the clothes he wore nor had heard him speak. They were in for something different. He walked flat-footed to the lectern in a pair of new boots that hurt his feet and wore a new but badly rumpled broadcloth suit that simply hung on him. His left hand clutched his lapel.

In a quaint dialect with a soft, high-pitched Kentucky twang, he said, "Mr. Cheerman."

Lincoln was so slow in getting started and seemed so ill at ease, the audience at first wavered between laughter and pity. In a short time, however, the sharp points of his address began to come and from that time on he held his audience spellbound.

54. Abraham Lincoln--taken June 3, 1860.

Throughout his speech, Lincoln spoke of the Southern slave holders. "We must not only let them alone, but we must somehow convince them that we do intend to let them alone. As wrong as we think it is, we can yet afford to let it alone where it is." Nevertheless, the Southern people took no stock in Lincoln's words. They judged him on a political basis as an abolitionist.

In conclusion, he said, "Let us have faith that right makes might and in that faith, let us to the end dare to do our duty as we understand it."

As he finished, the audience broke out in wild applause that lasted several minutes. That speech, along with the Lincoln-Douglas debates, did more to secure his nomination for the presidency than any other factor.

After the Cooper Union address, he accepted invitations to speak in several New England cities. That gave him an opportunity to spend a few days with his eldest son, Robert, a student at Phillips-Exeter Academy in Exeter, New Hampshire.

Lincoln's name became mentioned with increased frequency for the presidential nomination, with William H. Seward, former governor and then a senator from New York, his principal competitor. Seward was the acknowledged leader of the Republican Party.

The Republican Convention opened on May 16 in the Wigwam Building in Chicago. It could accommodate ten thousand people. Lincoln's name was placed into nomination by Norman B. Judd, chairman of the State Central Committee. The "Lincoln for President" committee was headed by the candidate's old friend, Judge Davis.

Seward had acquired hundreds of tickets to the convention for his supporters from the East. This left very few tickets for Lincoln's followers. Judge Davis contacted the printer, had several hundred duplicate tickets printed and gave them to the Lincoln men.

He advised them to enter the Wigwam as soon as the doors opened the next morning. Once inside, they were to yell loudly on a signal. Burton Cook, from Ottawa, was to take a handkerchief from his lapel pocket as a signal to start yelling and they were to keep it up until he put away the handkerchief. The Seward men who managed to squeeze into the building were, for the most part, drowned out by Cook and his men as the Westerners repeatedly shouted, "Lincoln! Lincoln! Lincoln!"

Lincoln had wired Judge Davis from Springfield, "Make no contracts that bind me." But the committee, in the candidate's absence, did bargain, cajole, coax, flatter and promise many things as the proceedings intensified.

The first ballot was 102 votes for Lincoln and 173-1/2 for Seward. On the third ballot, Lincoln was triumphantly nominated and Judge Davis rushed to wire him the good news. The nominee immediately went over to Eighth Street to share the good news with his wife. The ensuing rush of office seekers and other visitors forced him to take temporary quarters in the Statehouse in Springfield.

He neither wrote nor made any speeches after his nomination. (Contrast this with the high-powered, multimillion-dollar campaigns waged a century later.)

Lincoln was sure that his opponent's "Freeport Doctrine" had satisfied the Northern Democrats but in no way satisfied the Southern Democrats, almost assuring Douglas's defeat.

Douglas gave this appraisal of his opponent: "I shall have my hands full. Lincoln is the strong man of his party and the best stump speaker in the West. Of all the damned rascals about Springfield, Abe Lincoln is the ablest and the most honest." He also said, "Lincoln is a kind, amiable and intelligent gentleman, a good citizen and an honorable opponent."

In the final weeks of the campaign, Douglas abandoned the North to the Republicans and, in alarm at the growing talk of secession, made a tour of the slave states to plead for John Bell of Tennessee, the Southern Democratic candidate, who was pledged to maintain the Union. Lincoln carried all of the Northern states except New Jersey.

A few weeks after the "rail-splitter" candidate was elected, South Carolina seceded from the Union. A month after Lincoln's inauguration, hostilities began with the fall of Fort Sumter. The four years of war that followed coincided with Lincoln's four years as president.

Speaking of the war, he said:

"If the United States should fall, then free governments everywhere will have little chance of survival. If we fail, it will go far to prove the incapability of the people to govern themselves. Government of the people, by the people and for the people shall not perish from the earth."

By February 4, 1861, six Southern states had seceded from the Union. Their leaders met at Montgomery, Alabama, formed the Confederation of Southern States, drafted a constitution and elected Jefferson Davis president. The Southerners had no army or navy and very limited resources.

During his youth, Davis was educated in some of the finest schools in America, culminating with his graduation from the U. S. Military Academy at West Point. This was the opposite of Lincoln's education.

After leaving West Point, Davis enlisted as a second lieutenant in the infantry and participated in the Black Hawk War. Eleven years later, as a colonel, he distinguished himself for bravery in the war with Mexico and became an American hero in the North and South.

Davis had served in the U.S. House of Representatives and later became a U.S. Senator. He worked very hard to hold the Union together before the Southern states began seceding.

He had been appointed secretary of war under President Pierce and did much to update all facets of the U. S. Army, even to the point of experimenting in the desert of the Southwest with the possible use of camels by the military.

Lincoln traveled to Coles County to visit his stepmother. He rode in his buggy to Mattoon where he missed connections with a passenger train, so he traveled to Charleston in the caboose of a freight train. With a shawl over his shoulders and his boots covered with mud, Lincoln walked the length of the train to the station where a buggy was waiting.

He spent the night with his longtime friend and cousin, Dennis Hanks. The next morning, he rode in a buggy to southeast of Mattoon and stopped at the home of his stepsister, Matilda Johnston Moore, where his stepmother also lived. Much love and affection was shown between them.

They visited the old home place and the cemetery where his father was buried. He met many old friends and enjoyed his brief visit with them. The tears flowed freely as he embraced his stepmother for the last time. As they parted, he gave her his photograph--a picture of a son she cherished more than her own son.

55. Home of Matilda Johnston Moore, stepsister of Abraham Lincoln, located southeast of Mattoon, in Coles County, Illinois. President-elect visited his stepmother, Sarah Bush Johnston Lincoln, here, January 31, 1861.

There were two great problems facing the president-elect: forming a cabinet and drafting a policy for the South. Heavy pressure was exerted on him from all quarters. Not only was he elected by a minority of the voters, but there would be a majority in both Houses of Congress opposed to him. Even the U. S. Supreme Court's subsequent decisions seemed tainted with prejudice against him.

Grace Bedell, eleven, from Westfield, New York, suggested in a letter to the president-elect that he grow a beard, which he did. His beard, combined with his top hat, became his most readily recognizable features.

In early January, Mary journeyed to New York City where she bought several dresses for herself and a black silk hat for her husband. When she returned home, Lincoln said, "If nothing else comes of this scrape, we are going to get some new clothes."

On February 6, the Lincolns gave a farewell party for their friends. It was a triumphant affair for Mary, the new First Lady of the land. It was something she had struggled for through eighteen years of married life.

On Sunday afternoon, Lincoln visited with his law partner, William H. Herndon. As he left, he asked Herndon not to remove the shingle because he hoped to be back in business with him in the future.

Hundreds gathered at the station early in the morning on February 11 to bid him farewell. He gave a sad but eloquent address to the multitude that stood in a cold, drizzling rain.

"Pray that I may receive the Divine assistance, without which I cannot succeed, but with which, success is certain."

The train slowly left the station, taking Springfield's most prominent citizen to Washington, never to return again. A plot to assassinate Lincoln as he passed through Baltimore was averted by a change in plans.

Chapter 14
Washington, D.C. (1861)
War Between the States or
The Civil War

The family arrived in Washington on February 23, 1861 and took up residence at Willard's Hotel. On March 4, President James Buchanan came to escort Lincoln to the inaugural. They rode together down Pennsylvania Avenue in an open carriage.

As the president-elect approached the speaker's lectern, there was no place for his hat and cane. Senator Douglas realized the problem and rushed forward to remedy the situation.

When he returned to his seat in the fourth row, he said to Mary, "Well, if I can't be president, I can at least hold the president's hat and cane."

In his address, Lincoln appealed to the Southern people, declaring there was no intention of interfering with the institution of slavery in states where it already existed. He spoke against secession and ended his speech by extending a friendly hand to the Southern people.

Shortly after the inauguration, Douglas visited with his old friend and rival and assured him that he was fully prepared to support him at any cost to preserve the Union and maintain the federal government. He told Lincoln that he earlier had advised a large audience in Mobile, Alabama, that their rights would be much safer inside the Union than outside.

For Douglas, it was the last and most honorable service of his life. Illness ensued and, after a few weeks of suffering from typhoid fever, he died on June 3 in Chicago at the age of forty-eight. His last spoken words were, "Tell my sons to obey the law and uphold the Constitution of the United States." His death was mourned by the president.

In the final months of President Buchanan's term, treason had full liberty to accomplish its nefarious work in the capitol. Traitors in the cabinet and Congress conspired to deplete government resources, leaving it wholly unprepared to handle an emergency. The treasury was bankrupted deliberately; Navy ships were banished to distant ports; and Northern arsenals became a source of arms for rebels in states which had seceded. Through it all, Buchanan remained a passive spectator.

Following the inauguration, the first order of business for President Lincoln was to complete the selection and appointment of cabinet members. He discussed its composition with Vice President Hannibal Hamlin and they agreed it should have a geographical balance which was to include the South. Republican cabinet members selected were William H. Seward, New York, Secretary of State; Edward Bates, Missouri, Attorney General; and Caleb B. Smith, Indiana, Secretary of Interior. Former Democrats picked for the cabinet were Salmon P. Chase, Ohio, Secretary of Treasury; Montgomery Blair, Maryland, Postmaster General; Simon Cameron, Pennsylvania, Secretary of War; and Gideon Wells, Connecticut, Secretary of Navy.

When the president assumed the responsibility of the nation, he was not yet a great executive. However, he did not hesitate to surround himself with the most capable men available and he learned how to command them.

Painful experiment and the necessity of making difficult and immediate decisions taxed his brain to the utmost. He saved half of the border states for the Union at a time when, by a single mistake in timing or a harsh word, he might have lost them all to the Confederacy. His timely issuance of the Emancipation Proclamation gave the war an anti-slavery twist which forestalled a possibility of British intervention on behalf of the South.

From the time of Lincoln's election to the presidency, Seward, as the pre-Lincoln head of the party, assumed he would function as the nation's new administrator, with Lincoln being little more than a rubber stamp. On April 1, Seward attempted to advise Lincoln through a memorandum entitled "Some Thoughts for the President's Consideration," which included a possible declaration of war on Spain and France. Lincoln's oral reply to Seward left no doubt that he, as president, was the chief administrator and would make all final decisions.

Lincoln was told that his cabinet, all of whom thought themselves intellectually superior and more capable than the president, would "eat" him up. He replied, "They will be more likely to eat each other up." Horace Greeley, editor of the New York Tribune, also attempted to dictate presidential policy through his newspaper.

When the president tried to send food to the garrison at Fort Sumter, the Confederates regarded it as an act of war. At 4:30 in the morning on April 12, 1861, General Pierre Beauregard's batteries opened fire on the fort. That was the first shot of the Civil War or, as the Southerners referred to it, The War Between the States. Two days later, under Major Robert Anderson, the fort surrendered. Neither side lost a man, but it was the beginning of the bloodiest war the world had known up to that time. It was necessary for the president to issue a call to the loyal states for seventy-five thousand volunteers. That was one of the few times that the Northern states, as a block, rallied behind Lincoln.

The State of Virginia then seceded from the Union and joined the Southern Confederacy, which established its capitol at Richmond. That left Washington, D.C. in the very vulnerable position of being surrounded by Southern states and with no armed forces to protect it. As a result, Virginia became the chief battleground throughout the war.

On April 18, through an intermediary, Francis P. Blair, Lincoln offered General Robert E. Lee the command of the Northern Army. General Lee, a West Point graduate, was in command of the federal troops that captured John Brown at Harpers Ferry in 1859. He resigned his commission from the U. S. Army to join the Confederate forces.

Lee had no sympathy for secession and had opposed slavery, saying, "If I owned four million slaves I would sacrifice them to the Union, but how can I, as a loyal Virginian, fight against Virginia or draw my sword against my own sons?"

On November 1, the aged General Winfield Scott retired. Scott, who was known as "Old Fuss and Feathers," had been commander of the Union forces for several years. The president gave command of the military to George B. McClellan, a West Point graduate. He was most capable in terms of organization and training of troops. However, the president became disenchanted with him when he would win a battle and then not follow it up and finish the war. He always had an excuse. Lincoln relieved him of his command twice during the first part of the war.

McClellan's arrogance, hesitation, timidity and procrastination were his weaknesses. He even had the audacity to try to advise the president on how to operate the government. Once, after several months of inaction by General McClellan, Lincoln suggested that he should borrow the general's army and do something with it.

The president, whenever possible, gave his personal attention to the army camps around Washington. He felt close to the men and officers and mixed with them at every opportunity.

Virginia's secession placed the capital in great danger. There were no troops to guard or protect it until April 25 when the first regiment arrived from New York. Lincoln asked Congress, "Must a government, of necessity, be too strong for the liberties of its own people or too weak to maintain its own existence?"

No president has been associated with humor as much as Lincoln. The skill with which he could use an anecdote to illustrate a point was very helpful during times of great stress while he tried to work out problems with his cabinet. Some cabinet members did not always appreciate his humor. Lincoln consulted with his cabinet frequently and deferred to it many times. Nevertheless, he always made the final decision.

The first land skirmish was fought at Philippi, Virginia (now West Virginia). On June 2, a trainload of new Union volunteers from Ohio surprised an encampment of rebels. They killed several and took others as prisoners, but a few escaped into the woods. The western part of Virginia was cleared of armed rebels by the end of November. The first planned engagement in a land battle took place at Bull Run where the Confederates soundly defeated and routed the Union soldiers while civilians watched the shameful disaster.

Mary was in a very precarious position because she had a brother and a half-sister living in Lexington who were on the side of the North. One younger brother, three half-brothers and three half-sisters were sympathetic toward the South. One brother, D. H. Todd, became a lieutenant in the Confederate army.

A great tragedy struck at the White House when Willie died on February 20, 1862. He was the second son to be taken from the Lincolns and, added to the burden of the war, it seemed more than the family could bear. Tad was critically ill at the time and Mary was almost prostrate with grief and worry.

Mary always had hoped to be the mistress of the White House. She had dreamed of the day she would be at the top of the social ladder in Washington but when she entered that marble mansion in the

56. *President Lincoln visiting with General George B. McCellan, commander of the Army of the Potomac, at the Antietam battlefield, October 3, 1862.*

spring of 1861, she became its most lonely figure. Her sharp tongue and quick temper allowed her very few friends. Her dressmaker, Mrs. Elizabeth Keckley, a lifelong friend, was a mulatto woman who once had been the dressmaker for Mrs. Jefferson Davis.

Lincoln had difficulty securing military leaders capable of coping with the tactics of General Lee. Congress and the public clamored for victories. That pressure forced the president to issue military orders and dictate strategy, though he recognized his lack of military knowledge. After July 11, Lincoln put General Halleck in command of the Union armies, succeeding McClellan. The supreme control of war policies then shifted directly into the hands of the president.

Taney, a Southerner, was Chief Justice of the U. S. Supreme Court when Lincoln took office. It was Taney who had handed down the Dred Scott decision in 1857. He was hostile toward the president and openly defied him. However, when Congress increased the size of the court to ten, it gave Lincoln the opportunity to appoint his longtime friend, Judge David Davis, to the high court in 1862. Davis had been Lincoln's manager at the Chicago Convention in 1860.

Things were going so badly for the Union in the fall of 1862 that Secretary of the Treasury Chase tried to demonstrate a way for the entire cabinet to depart at once. Seward, Chase and Stanton tendered their letters of resignation. Lincoln accepted only Chase's letter, saying, "I now have a balanced load."

Lincoln's compassion for his fellow men was evident in his excessive use of the executive power to pardon. He often suspended death sentences imposed upon soldiers by court-martial for falling asleep while on sentry duty. Lincoln said that a live soldier was worth a "heap" more than a dead one. It also avoided the grief, sorrow and humiliation which would be suffered by the soldier's family.

Lincoln's inability to persuade his generals to take advantage of a critical situation was frustrating. After Lee's army suffered disastrous losses when it was defeated at Gettysburg, Lee retreated south but was stopped by the flood waters of the Potomac River. Lee was in a trap and his supply line was blocked.

Lincoln thought General Meade should have taken advantage of the situation by seizing upon a golden opportunity to capture Lee's army and end the war. He urged Meade to follow and attack Lee with all haste. Instead, Meade found excuses for not carrying through. He hesitated, procrastinated and refused to attack. Finally, the waters receded, allowing Lee and his army to escape from a very critical situation.

Lincoln was furious. He wrote Meade a blistering letter but did not mail it. Writing the letter at least had the effect of relieving part of the president's frustration. Meade suggested his own resignation.

During his presidency, Lincoln signed into law four bills of long-lasting importance to the nation's physical and natural environment. When the war began, inhabitants of the western part of Virginia refused to secede from the North. Lincoln signed a bill on June 20, 1863, establishing West Virginia as a separate state. It was the only state to secede from the South during the conflict.

On September 28, he proclaimed the last Thursday of November as Thanksgiving Day.

In 1864, he signed a bill to protect and preserve the area now known as Yosemite National Park. This area, located in the High Sierra of California, was destined to become the first park of its kind.

After California was admitted to the Union in 1850, its missions gradually fell into ruin from vandalism and neglect. It was less than a month before his assassination that Lincoln signed a decree transferring their ownership to the Catholic Church. Since then, a gradual restoration of the missions has taken place.

Chapter 15
Emancipation Proclamation

President Lincoln issued his final draft of the Emancipation Proclamation on January 1, 1863. It was a great day for the slaves in the South, because it gave them their freedom on January 31, 1865, constitutionally abolishing slavery. The Thirteenth Amendment was passed before the year was out and the president also granted amnesty to "all persons" taking an oath to uphold and support the Constitution of the United States.

On January 29, General Grant was put in command of the army of the West, with orders to capture Vicksburg, the last Confederate stronghold on the Mississippi. The president said, "The war can never be brought to a close until Vicksburg is ours."

Grant cut all supply lines to the city and starved its inhabitants into submission. It took seven weeks of siege and heavy bombardment before General John C. Pemberton asked for terms of surrender. General Grant's reply was, "Unconditional."

Grant ordered his quartermaster to feed the starving people, civilians and military alike, because Vicksburg's food supply had been exhausted several days earlier. They had been reduced to living in caves and subsisting on horse meat and rats.

During a five-day period on the march to Vicksburg, Grant did not have a horse, orderly, blanket, overcoat or clean clothes. For weeks, his soldiers lived off the land. They took their food and supplies from the farming section where they were fighting. They once marched 180 miles and fought five battles in twenty days to reach Vicksburg. In the same city, the first Negro troops fought against the whites of the South.

After Grant's terrible loss of troops in the bloody battle at Shiloh, public opinion turned against him. Many letters reached the White House complaining about that cigar-chewing, heavy-drinking, sloppily clothed general and asking the president to get rid of him. Lincoln asked one complaining doctor, "What brand does the general drink? I would like to have the other generals drink the same brand. I can't spare this man; he fights!"

The turning point of the war for the Union was the defeat of the Confederates at Gettysburg, followed the next day, July 4, by the surrender of Vicksburg. Grant had placed the entire Mississippi River in the hands of the North and split the Confederacy at the same time.

Lincoln received an invitation to the dedication ceremony at Gettysburg Cemetery but was not asked to speak. Some thought he was not qualified to do so at such a momentous occasion. Nevertheless, in accepting the invitation, he asked if he could make a few appropriate remarks.

Edward Everett, the foremost American orator of the day and former president of Harvard University, had been selected as the speaker. On November 19, 1863, Everett spoke without a flaw for two hours. Contrast that with Lincoln's 271 words which took about two minutes.

The depressed president thought his few words were a failure and so did many newspaper editors. Little did they know that those few words would be remembered far longer than those spoken so eloquently by Everett.

A few days later, Everett wrote a letter to the president, saying, "I should be glad if I could flatter myself that I came as near to the central idea of the occasion in two hours as you did in two minutes." The Gettysburg Address is now considered one of the great speeches of all time.

Lincoln was a light sleeper and rose early each morning. He saw visitors by the hundreds and held cabinet meetings Tuesday and Friday afternoons.

He was asked to pardon many a soldier who was to be shot for desertion or other acts of treason. To one crying mother's plea, he said, "Well, I don't believe shooting your son will do him any good. Hand me that pen."

On another occasion, Lincoln said, "Must I shoot a simple-minded soldier boy who deserts, while I must not touch a hair of the wily agitator who induced him to do so?"

Lincoln's ratings among the more respectable and influential people of the North sank to the lowest point since his election. There were indications of a secret movement to impeach him.

To add insult to injury, someone took a shot at him one evening as he was riding his horse from the White House to the Soldiers Home where he was living at the time. The next morning, a servant found

57. *Wax figures of President Lincoln and his two secretaries, John Nicolay and John Hay -- Located in Gettysburg,*

the president's hat lying alongside the trail, with a bullet hole through the top.

In early 1864, not one senator in Washington was thought to be favorable toward Lincoln's renomination. His fitness for the presidency was much in question. The one bright spot in the president's life was his young son, Tad. They were chums and Tad usually slept with his father.

He would charge into his father's office without warning, sometimes cracking a whip and driving two goats hitched to a kitchen chair. All children felt at ease with the president and he always had a kind word and a handshake for each youngster.

In February, Lincoln had appointed Major General Ulysses S. Grant to head the Union forces.

Grant previously had captured Fort Henry and Fort Donelson, but he was little known until the siege at Vicksburg. He was a graduate of West Point with average grades and took part in the war with Mexico where he first met General Lee. He resigned from the army and was broke when he and his family arrived in St. Louis.

He tried farming for a short time but finally became a clerk in his father's hardware and leather store in Galena, Illinois. After the fall of Fort Sumter, he tried to get a military appointment but was unsuccessful. Later, he was appointed a colonel in the 21st Illinois Infantry.

On March 10, 1864, Lincoln personally handed Grant his new commission as lieutenant general, the highest army rank at that time. Only General Washington previously had held this high rank.

Grant's overall strategy was to hit Lee from three fronts: General Sherman from the south, General Sheridan from the west and his own troops from the north. Grant's first order to his generals was to follow Lee whenever and wherever he went. Lincoln felt confident that Grant could quickly bring the war to a successful conclusion.

Lincoln knew that no words, explanation, persuasion, letters or speeches could serve his cause. Only bayonets dripping with Confederate blood and defeat of the South could bring about his reelection. He believed that the Almighty would see him through.

"Without His assistance, I cannot succeed; with His assistance I cannot fail," he said. Scripture reading and prayer were in his daily routine and he believed that when all else failed it was time for a person to get down on his knees.

The first good news to reach the president in quite awhile came from General Sherman, who wired, "Atlanta is ours!" By Christmas, he had taken Savannah. Next was General Sheridan's success in the Shenandoah Valley of Virginia.

The house where John Lincoln (President Lincoln's distant cousin) was born in 1824 was destroyed a few weeks before the war ended. Because of this, John hated the president until his death. General Sheridan's raid wiped out most of the homes along Linville Creek in the Shenandoah Valley. Many other relatives of Lincoln had voted against him and fought for the Confederacy.

The South now was surrounded completely by a blockade and its last recruits, young and old, had been activated. Its armies were losing an average of one regiment a day through desertion and the South's cause was beginning to look hopeless.

Lincoln's campaign opponents said, "The war was a failure" and blamed him. They criticized his strong emergency measures, such as suspension of the right of habeas corpus, as unconstitutional.

On October 12, 1864, Justice Taney, eighty-five, died and the president named former Secretary of Treasury Salmon P. Chase to succeed him. Lincoln, for the first time, now had a branch of the federal government working for him instead of against him.

Sherman started his devastating march through Georgia on November 15. His army outdistanced its supply line and was forced to live entirely off the land. Any supplies they could not eat or carry were destroyed. It was a scorched-earth policy for railroads, buildings, crops and livestock. Nothing was left behind to aid anyone's survival.

In Congress, the radicals in the president's own party tried to formulate a scheme to remove him from office. The break between the president and his adversaries was now complete and Lincoln saw no way for his reelection. Yet, when the National Union Party Convention met, Lincoln was named on the first ballot. He carried every state except Missouri. Andrew Johnson, a Democrat from Tennessee, was nominated for the vice presidency in recognition of his work for the Union.

Newspapers violently attacked Lincoln. His Democratic opponent was General McClellan, who earlier could not win a war but felt qualified to tell the president how to run the government.

The election's outcome was 213 electoral votes for Lincoln and twenty-one for McClellan. The results proved that, despite the long and bloody war, the people of the North were resolved to see it through to the finish.

The prison camp at Andersonville, Georgia, came to the attention of the people in the North and they were outraged to hear of the inhumane treatment of captured Union soldiers. Altogether, 8,589 prisoners died within a four-month period from starvation, disease and filth. Pressure was put on the president to treat the captured Confederate soldiers in the same manner, but he could not be so cruel.

The South was now in a desperate situation and it was getting worse each day. Confederate money was almost worthless and manpower and resources were desperately low.

Often Lee would send men and wagons into the countryside to search for food and they would come back with nothing. On the other hand, the North had gained steadily in all aspects of the war, including food supplies, manufacturing, transportation and, most important, manpower.

In December, Princeton College conferred a doctorate-of-law degree upon Lincoln. This was an exceptional honor for someone who had less than one year of formal schooling.

Jefferson Davis was so jealous of his constitutional rights as commander in chief that he was reluctant to give General Lee full command of all the Confederate armies until early 1865. For the Southerners, that was probably four years too late because now their cause seemed lost.

On January 29, President Davis sent a committee to Fort Monroe to present a proposal for peace. Anything less than unconditional surrender was unacceptable to the North, so the struggle continued.

Charleston, South Carolina, was captured by Sherman's Union forces on February 22. That was the place where the war had started four years earlier when Fort Sumter was attacked. Charleston's surrender brought humiliation and disgrace for the elite of the city.

Lincoln, at his second inaugural on March 4, said, "With malice toward none; with charity for all; with firmness in the right, as God gave us to see the right, let us strive on to finish the work we are in." Upon reaching the great plaza in front of the Capitol, Lincoln reread his inaugural address to the multitude waiting there. It was received in profound silence.

At the inaugural ball, the president shook hands with more than six thousand well-wishers. Frederick Douglass, a Negro leader, was detained by a policeman at the door. When he learned of this, Lincoln sent for Douglass and shook his hand cordially. Mary was at the president's side in the reception line, dressed in the finest of imported European fabric.

Along with his other difficult problems, Lincoln had to contend with his wife and her many faults. She was often tactless and meddled in the affairs of others. She was very jealous of every female her husband would converse with or acknowledge. She always complained about and criticized her husband, saying, "He is too stoop-shouldered and walks awkwardly." She irritated him constantly.

One evening, shortly after their marriage, they were eating supper at the boarding house in Springfield. Mary became enraged at her husband and threw a cup of hot coffee into his face. He sat there motionless, not saying a word, while Mrs. Early, the landlady, wiped his face with a towel.

Lincoln tried to avoid his wife whenever possible. Once when the Grants were visiting the White House, Mary shouted at the general's wife, "How dare you be seated in my presence until I invite you!"

Some say Lincoln's greatest tragedy was not his assassination but his marriage. However, Mary was a good mother and a loyal and faithful wife, despite her many faults.

One afternoon, the president planned a review of the Union army. He rode in a carriage with Generals Grant and Ord. Mary and Mrs. Grant followed in an ambulance. When Mary saw that Mrs. Ord was riding with the president, she exploded.

"What does that woman mean riding by the side of the president and ahead of me?" When the review was over, she gave Mrs. Ord a terrible tongue-lashing. At the same time, she attacked her husband in the presence of officers and others for allowing it to happen. Lincoln sat motionless and bore it as a saint might have done.

On March 27, Lincoln met with Generals Grant and Sherman and Admiral Porter on the steamer River Queen at City Point on the James River. In discussing the possible ending of the war, Grant and Sherman believed there would be one more battle--the last. Lincoln hoped it could be avoided, but the generals said, "It will be mainly Lee's choice." They spoke of terms of surrender and how the South should be treated after the war.

On April 1, Grant maneuvered his army around Lee's right flank and captured Petersburg. The next day, Richmond, the Confederate capitol, was evacuated by Davis and his cabinet.

Two days later, Lincoln rode almost unattended in a carriage through the streets of Richmond. One Negro shouted, "Glory, hallelujah!" and fell to his knees. Lincoln said to him, "Don't kneel to me. You must kneel to God only and thank Him for your freedom."

As the president rode through the city, General Godfrey Weitzel asked him what he should do with the conquered people? Lincoln replied, "If I were in your place, I'd let 'em up easy."

General Lee wrote to President Davis, "I fear it will be impossible to prevent the junction of Grant and Sherman's armies." But Davis still held the hope there was a way for the South to succeed.

Lee's army raced westward to Amelia Court House where he had hoped to find food and supplies but, to his great disappointment, there were none. The plight of his soldiers, dressed in ragged uniforms and wearing worn-out shoes, was desperate but, worst of all, there was no food.

On April 8, Grant sent a message to Lee demanding his surrender. The next morning, Lee found he was completely surrounded by the armies of Sheridan, Ord, Griffin and Grant. There was nothing left for him to do but go to see Grant. He sent a note asking for a conference. Grant set the place at Appomattox Court House in Major Wilmer McLean's house.

The major had owned a farm on Bull Run where the Battle of Bull Run occurred at the beginning of the war. He moved from there, thinking he would escape the conflict. He now found himself as host to the signing of the surrender.

58. *Reconstructed - Major Wilmer McLean's house in Appomattox Court House, Virginia, where General Lee met with General Grant to arrange a surrender, ending the Civil War or the War between the States.*

59. General Robert E. Lee surrenders his Confederate Army to General Ulysses Grant on Palm Sunday, April 9, 1865. General Grant telegraphed the good news to President Lincoln that afternoon.

Lee came in an immaculate uniform, but Grant's was ill-kept and splashed with mud.   After a few words of personal exchange, Lee asked about the terms of surrender.

Grant replied, "All officers and men surrendering are to be paroled and relieved of all of their arms and ammunitions."

Lee nodded his acceptance.

Grant asked Lee if he had any requests and Lee said, "Yes, I have. Some of my men own their horses and should be allowed to keep them, as they are sorely needed for spring plowing." Grant agreed and Lee made a grateful acknowledgment for the concession. Grant then issued orders to his quartermaster to feed Lee's starving army.

A last bloody battle, which the president dreaded, had been avoided.   The war was over and the Union was safe.   Grant, in keeping with the president's spirit, asked his men to refrain from any celebration and said, "The war is over; the rebels are our fellow countrymen again." On April 9, Palm Sunday, Grant telegraphed the president at 4:30 in the afternoon that Lee had surrendered.

After Lincoln spoke to the large number of people who had gathered, Senator Harlan asked them, "What shall we do with these rebels?"

"Hang them! Hang them!" the crowd shouted.

Little Tad, standing at his father's side, said, "No, no, Papa. Not hang them. Hang onto them."

Lincoln cried out happily, "We must hang onto them! I love the Southern people more than they love me. My greatest desire is to restore the Union. Don't criticize them. We would have acted the same as they did under similar circumstances."

The concern for Negro slaves was nothing new to the Lincoln family. It started with Levi Lincoln, born in 1749 in Hingham. He was a great-great-grandson of Samuel and a distant relative of President Lincoln. He was a Harvard graduate, studied law and served with the minutemen at Cambridge in the Lexington battle in April 1775. He was admitted to the bar and was very successful. He became attorney general under President Thomas Jefferson. He was appointed later as lieutenant governor of the State of Massachusetts and an associate justice of the U. S. Supreme Court.

He wrote a brief involving Negro slaves, basing his argument on the law of the nature of God.   He said that no man in the State of Massachusetts could claim to be the master of another and that all men were, in truth, born free.   The result was that slavery was abolished in Massachusetts.   About eighty years later, another descendent of Samuel s, President Lincoln, had just emerged from the midst of a great civil war which forever abolished slavery in the United States.

As a U. S. Senator before the war, Jefferson Davis stood for states' rights.   That very well could have cost him the war, because each state tried to go its own separate way.   As the war progressed, Davis took more and more power from the Southern states, until even his own cabinet complained there was more personal freedom in Washington than in Richmond.

Davis was a very articulate man who tried to conduct the war by issuing a great volume of orders from his desk in Richmond.   He did not want to relinquish any power to any general who might have done a better job.   He also seemed to be fighting a holding or defensive war.

Lincoln was just the opposite.   He always urged his generals to pursue the enemy.   He was not so much interested in occupying the land as he was in defeating the Confederates.

When the war began, Lincoln had no previous experience in military fighting and, during the first three years, he was unable to find a general who would follow through.   He was forced to educate himself in the art of warfare to such an extent that some historians believe that if he and Davis had switched sides, it is quite likely the South would have been victorious.

There is one other thought.   If General Lee could have found it possible to accept Lincoln's offer to command the Union army, the war might have been over in a few months.   Lee was a genius at tactical warfare and every rebel soldier would have laid down his life for him.

The South had many difficulties at the outset of the war.   It had very few manufacturing plants and no finances to construct them. Transportation was limited and most of the ports were blockaded almost from the beginning.

Added to this was the lack of an army or navy and a much smaller population to draw from.   It makes one wonder how the conflict lasted more than a year. It could have been the brilliance, expertise and willpower of General Lee.

Now that the war was over, Lincoln spent much of his time devising a plan for reconstruction of the South. He also discussed with Mary their travel plans abroad and how they would settle in Springfield after his term was up.

Lincoln's whole feeling toward the Southern people was one of peace and magnanimity. While many were clamoring for the execution of the rebel leaders, especially Jefferson Davis, Lincoln said only a day or two before his assassination "This talk about Mister Davis tires me. I hope he will mount a fleeting horse, reach the shores of the Gulf of Mexico and drive so far into its waters that we shall never see him again."

Then he told a pat story--perhaps his last--of a boy in Springfield "who saved up his money and bought a coon which, after the novelty wore off, became a great nuisance. One day, he was leading him through the streets and had his hands full to keep clear of the little hellion, who had torn his clothes half off of him. At length, he sat down on the curbstone, completely fagged out. A man passing was stopped by the lad's disconsolate appearance and asked what was the matter.

"'Oh, this coon is such a trouble to me.'

"'Why don't you get rid of him, then?' asked the gentleman.

"'Hush,' said the boy, 'don't you see he is gnawing his rope off? I am going to let him do it and then I will go home and tell the folks that he got away from me.'"

60. Last known photograph, from life, of President Lincoln, made April 10, 1865, five days before his assassination.

Chapter 16
President's Assassination--Interments

On Good Friday, April 14, 1865, Major General Robert Anderson, who had surrendered Fort Sumter four years earlier, hoisted the Union flag once again at the fort. On the same day, General Grant arrived in Washington and the Union military draft was stopped. Lincoln met with his cabinet in the afternoon and, after dinner, took Mary to the Ford Theater to see a play called "Our American Cousin."

Shortly after 9:30 that evening, John Wilkes Booth, an actor and Southern sympathizer, entered the president's box through a rear door and shot him. Booth jumped about eleven feet to the stage below, breaking a leg but still able to make his escape from the theater.

Dr. Charles Leal, who was in the theater, examined the wound and saw it was mortal. Lincoln was carried across the street and placed on a bed in Mr. Peterson's rooming house at 453 Tenth Street where he struggled with death for approximately ten hours. At 7:22 the next morning, he breathed his last and then he belonged to the ages.

As Lincoln lay dying, Secretary of War Stanton said, "Here lies the most perfect ruler of men that the world has ever seen."

Just six days after Lee's surrender, the president was dead. His death was a great loss for the whole nation, especially the war-torn South. Lincoln had wanted the South back into the Union on the easiest possible terms, but now his work was finished and others would dictate terms to the vanquished.

At the time of the president's assassination, one of the conspirators attempted to murder Secretary of State Seward and another unsuccessfully tried to kill Vice President Johnson.

Lincoln's body lay in state in the East Room of the White House and then in the Capitol rotunda. Once, while viewing the coffin in the White House, Tad, with tears streaming down his face, said, "If Papa would have lived, he would have forgiven the man who shot him. Papa forgave everybody."

On April 21, the bodies of Lincoln and his son, Willie, were placed aboard a special train to Springfield. During the slow journey across the nation, approximately seven million Americans viewed the coffin

61. Wax figures of President Lincoln and his wife, Mary, as they sat in the Ford Theater, April 14, 1865. John Wilkes Booth shot the President at about 9:30 PM.

and more than 1.5 million saw his face. Father and son were interred in the Oak Ridge Cemetery in Springfield on May 4, 1865. When Lincoln's stepmother, Sarah was notified, she said, "I knowed when he went away he'd never come back alive."

Of the eight conspirators, four were hanged, three were put in prison, one fled the country and Booth was shot while trying to hide in a burning barn. He died shortly afterward near Port Royal, Virginia and was secretly buried in a swamp along the Potomac. He was reburied in Baltimore, MD in 1869.

Jefferson Davis was captured in Georgia and spent two years imprisoned at Fort Monroe, Virginia, before being released. General Lee continued to help make his country a union of loyal states once more. While doing this, he was named president of the Washington College in Lexington, Virginia. After his death, it was renamed Washington and Lee University. He was buried in a mausoleum in the chapel, a fitting resting place for a truly great man.

Lincoln's burial did not end concern for the safety of his body. In 1876, intruders planning to demand a $200,000 ransom broke into the sepulcher of the Lincoln Monument, smashed the president's sarcophagus and attempted to remove the casket. They were frightened away, but not before bullets had ricocheted off the tomb's marble walls. The intruders were apprehended later in Chicago and sentenced to one year in prison.

Fearing another kidnap attempt, Robert had his father's body secreted away in the tomb's vast recesses, even hiding it once under a pile of lumber. It took twenty-five years to construct his final resting place.

On September 26, 1901, Robert went to Springfield and made final arrangements for the reinterment of his mother and father; his three brothers, Eddie, Willie and Tad; and his own son, Abraham III. Lincoln's body was placed in a case of flat steel bars resting on twenty inches of cement and covered with two tons of concrete, ten feet below the surface of the ground.

Before departing, Robert left instructions that the coffin was not to be opened. However, friends handling the arrangements decided, in Robert's absence, that the casket should be opened for a final visual inspection to make sure it was Lincoln's body in the red cedar box.

62. *Lincoln Memorial located on the bank of the Potomac River, in Washington, D.C., taken from atop the Washington Monument.*

63. Marble statue of President Lincoln enclosed within the Lincoln Memorial in Washington, D.C.

As the lead encasement was chiseled away from the top of the coffin, people gathered around to view Lincoln's face for the last time. In that group was Fleetwood Lindley, thirteen. In 1963, Lindley, then a man of seventy-five, was believed to be the last known person alive who saw Lincoln's face.

A few days before his death that year, Lindley described Lincoln's features as entirely recognizable and the expression as one of sadness. The whiskers, which had been dusted with white chalk by the undertaker, the black bow tie and the wart on his right cheek were unmistakably Abraham Lincoln's. His eyebrows had vanished and the new, black broadcloth suit which the president had worn at his second inaugural was partially covered with yellow mold. When everyone was satisfied it was Lincoln's body, the coffin lid was closed to mortal eyes for the last time. Although he is no longer visible, he will live on forever in the hearts of the American people.

Lincoln might be compared to Moses, who, as a baby, was found in the bulrushes along the Nile and became the great Hebrew leader to whom God gave a command. Moses led his people out of Egypt, the land of bondage, then spent forty years in the wilderness seeking the land of milk and honey. Moses died shortly before his people reached the promised land, but the commandments brought moral and spiritual light to the world.

Lincoln was born into poverty and the lowest of circumstances, but with a God-given desire to take the Negro slaves out of their bondage. Although Lincoln was able to save the Union, he, too, was unable to see in his lifetime the land of promise with complete freedom for the slaves. Shortly before his plans could be formulated and put into practice, he was assassinated. But, as with Moses, his ideals are slowly being carried out and one day there will be equality for all in this land of the free and home of the brave.

64　Final resting place for President Lincoln and his family, except his oldest son, Robert Todd Lincoln. President Lincoln's

65. Lincoln Tomb, constructed in 1901, in the Oak Ridge Cemetery, Springfield, Illinois.

Chapter 17
Mary Todd Lincoln's Later Life

After Lincoln's assassination, his wife, Mary, spent the next seventeen years in torment, shame and disgrace unequaled before or since by a president's widow.

She was accused of stealing things from the White House when she vacated the mansion. It took her five weeks of packing before moving to Chicago. On the morning she left Washington, no one was there to say good-bye. Mary owed approximately seventy thousand dollars and was forced to live in a rooming house. The only kind thing related to the president's death was that he died without knowing of Mary's huge indebtedness.

Mary became so paranoid that she made a spectacle of herself in public and generated national gossip. While in Chicago, she tried to persuade Congress to give her $100,000, which it refused to do. Later, she was given $25,000 and she bought a house. Before long, her money was gone and for awhile she provided room and board for others. In a short time, she lost her home to creditors and she, in turn, moved into a boarding house.

Mary was so destitute in 1867 that she packed several boxes of her old dresses and jewelry, went to New York City and tried to sell them. The clothing was practically worthless. She then asked for contributions, bringing disgrace to her family and now she was to be pitied.

Mary was not on speaking terms with any of her sisters and finally broke with her son, Robert. She now had only one friend left, her former dressmaker, Mrs. Keckley, but she lived in New York.

In 1868, the Fourteenth Amendment was signed into law, giving the Negroes their citizenship. In 1870, the Fifteenth Amendment gave them the right to vote.

In April 1869, Lincoln's stepmother, Sarah Bush Johnston Lincoln, died and was buried beside her husband in Shiloh Cemetery.

Finally, Lincoln's estate was settled and Mary and her two living sons received $36,765 each. She took Tad abroad for a couple of years and lived in solitude. When the money was gone, she was back in Chicago pleading poverty and the U. S. Senate granted her a $3,000 annual pension.

Up to this point, all Mary had to live for was her son, Tad, but he died of typhoid fever in 1871. Mary was now completely alone, friendless and in despair. She was so unstable that Robert had the courts declare her insane and she was confined in a private asylum at Batavia, Illinois. After thirteen months, Mary was released but, unfortunately, she was not cured.

Mary spent another few years abroad in Pau, France, not letting Robert know where she was. While there, she fell and injured her spinal cord and was unable to walk for a time.

Her final days were spent in semi-darkness in the home of her sister, Elizabeth Edwards, in Springfield where she had married forty years earlier. Mary died July 16, 1882, following a paralytic stroke, ending a pitiful saga which might have been so different, considering her many attributes, if only her personality had been different.

Chapter 18
Abraham Lincoln's Descendants
Through 1985

Robert Todd Lincoln, born in a boarding house in Springfield on August 1, 1843, was the only son who lived to maturity. He graduated from Harvard University in 1864 and was commissioned a captain in the U. S. Army and assigned to General Grant's staff. He was present at Appomattox when General Lee surrendered.

On September 14, 1868, Robert married Mary Harlan, whose father was a senator and one of the prominent founders of the Republican Party.

Robert became a successful attorney in Chicago and was appointed secretary of war (1881-85) by President Garfield. He also served as minister to Great Britain (1889-93) under President Harrison. For several years, Robert was considered seriously as a potential presidential candidate. Each time, however, the move was stopped because he refused to run.

Robert was chosen president and, later, chairman of the board of the Pullman Company headquartered in Chicago. He was a very successful businessman and was the controlling factor in several large corporations. He became a millionaire in his own right.

In 1902, Robert and Mary began construction on Hildene, an elegant mansion, as a summer home. It was located on 412 acres in the mountains of Vermont on the outskirts of Manchester. Robert had visited Manchester in the summers of 1863 and 1864 with his mother and his younger brother, Tad. His father was to have vacationed there with the family the following summer.

Just one year before President Lincoln was assassinated, Robert was almost killed. He was pulled from beneath a train at the Jersey City depot by Edwin Booth, a brother of John Wilkes Booth. Robert had been jostled accidentally from the station platform onto the tracks in the path of an approaching train.

In April 1865, Robert removed all of his father's papers from the White House and they were sealed from public view for eighty-two years. From 1910 until 1919, he took eight trunks of those papers with him in a special baggage car wherever he went. He then gave them to the Library of Congress with the stipulation that no one was to see them until twenty-one years after his death. Robert reportedly had burned valuable papers before his death, possibly those concerning his mother's mental illness.

Robert participated in the dedication ceremonies of the Lincoln Memorial in 1922. He was the only person who had some association with all four presidential assassinations. He was at his father's bedside when he died in 1865 and he was walking with President Garfield at the Washington railway station when an assassin's bullet found its mark. Twenty years later, Robert had just stepped off the train at Buffalo, New York, as President McKinley was shot and mortally wounded.

After the death of President McKinley, Robert, fearing he was a jinx, refused to accept any invitations which would put him in the same vicinity as a president. Ironically, Robert's grave is just a few hundred feet from that of President John F. Kennedy in Arlington National Cemetery. Robert Todd Lincoln died on July 26, 1926, at Hildene, just six days before his eighty-third birthday.

Robert and Mary had a family of three--Mary, Abraham III and Jessie. Mary was born on October 15, 1869 and married Charles Isham, her father's secretary, on September 2, 1891, in London, England. They had one child, Lincoln Isham, born in 1892, who died childless in 1971.

Abraham III was born on August 14, 1873 and died of blood poisoning at the age of seventeen on March 5, 1890, in London, England. He was reinterred with his grandfather in Springfield in 1901.

Jessie, their last child, was born on November 6, 1875 and died in 1948. Her first marriage, on November 10, 1897, was an elopement with Warren Beckwith, who was born in 1873 and died in 1955. That marriage ended in divorce in 1907.

She was married twice after that, in 1915 to Frank Johnson and then to Robert Randolph in 1926. Two children were born during her first marriage: Mary Lincoln Beckwith, born on August 22, 1898 and Robert Todd Lincoln Beckwith, born on July 19, 1904 in Riverside, Illinois.

Mary Beckwith was unmarried and had no offspring. At the request of the U. S. Navy in 1960, she launched the nuclear-powered submarine Abraham Lincoln. In 1975, Mary died at Hildene, thus ending the Lincoln family's reign in the great mansion. She was the mistress at Hildene for thirty-seven years. It is now a national historic site.

Robert Beckwith received a law degree from the National University in Washington, D.C. Robert was interested in sailing, raising cattle and automobile racing.

He and his first wife, Hazel Wilson, were married for thirty years and had no children. Three years after her death, Robert married his housekeeper, Annamarie Hoffman, twenty-six, on November 6, 1967.

Prior to his marriage to Annamarie, Robert had undergone a therapeutic prostate operation and a vasectomy which left him sterile, according to medical testimony. When he learned of his wife's pregnancy six months later, he separated from her. A son, Timothy Lincoln Beckwith, was born on October 14, 1968, in the Community Hospital in Williamsburg, Virginia. Shortly afterward, Annamarie returned with her son to West Berlin, Germany, her former home.

In a divorce suit filed on October 30, 1973, Robert claimed he did not father the boy and that the child's birth proved his wife had been adulterous. Annamarie had signed an affidavit stating her husband was not the father of her child, but later she repudiated the claim, saying it was signed under duress.

On March 10, 1975, Superior Court Judge Joseph Ryan, Jr. ordered that she be given one thousand dollars for travel expenses and three thousand dollars for attorney fees on the condition that blood tests be made in Germany and sent to the United States to aid the court in arriving at the truth. Annamarie asked the court to strike out the requirement for the blood test, contending it would violate the boy's right to privacy. The blood tests were never received.

Robert was granted a divorce on August 3, 1976, by Judge Ryan on the grounds of adultery.

In 1981, Robert married Margaret Fristoe. They lived very comfortably in Saluda, Virginia. Margaret, sixty-three, was very much interested in Hildene. Robert, in frail health but very much alert, was the last descendant of Abraham Lincoln, our sixteenth president. He died on December 24, 1985.

Since there has been no proven blood line beyond Robert, the Lincoln trust of more than one million dollars was, according to the will of Mary Harlan Lincoln, divided equally among the Christian Science Church in Boston, the American National Red Cross and Iowa Wesleyan College.

Chapter 19
Looking Back

Out of seven generations of Lincolns, which included the president, only Mordecai I was born, married and died in the same state. In two more generations, the cycle closed. Robert Lincoln, the only son of the president to reach maturity, died in New England, not far from where Samuel Lincoln had landed in 1637.

In nine generations, the Lincolns had crossed the Atlantic, settled in New England and established homes in Massachusetts, New Jersey, Pennsylvania, Virginia, Kentucky, Indiana, Illinois, Washington, D.C. and then back to New England.

It is an interesting coincidence that the last male member of the family, Abraham III (Robert Lincoln's only son), died in England, the country where his ancestors originated. At his death, he was nearly eighteen, the same age as Samuel Lincoln when he left England nearly three centuries earlier.

Chapter 20

Conclusion

Intermarriages between the Boone and Lincoln families in Berks County were still in process as recent as 1906, when Harry Boone of Stonerville in Exeter Township married Bertha Lincoln of Reading.

On November 11, 1938, the Daniel Boone Homestead in Berks County was dedicated and opened to the public. The Cumberland Gap National Park was authorized and established in 1955. Fort Bonnesborough was rebuilt and opened to the public on August 30, 1974.

Many who have studied the life of Daniel Boone think his proper burial place should have been at Fort Boonesborough. If Daniel Boone could have chosen his final resting place in Kentucky, he surely would have chosen Boonesborough where he and Becky spent most of their time while in Kentucky.

About the Author

Willard Mounts was born in the Appalachian Mountains of West Virginia where he swung on grape vines on the banks of the Tug River which borders Kentucky. This area is noted as the home of the famous Hatfield and McCoy feud. The author is part McCoy.

Mounts grew up during the Depression. His father was a coal miner living in coal camps, where de-licing was a weekly chore and bedbugs and rats were a constant menace.

During his late teens, he attended a military camp for three summers at Fort Knox, Kentucky. While there, he visited Abraham Lincoln's birthplace near Hodgenville and the Nall Cemetery where Lincoln's grandmother, Bathsheba, is buried. Those visits created a desire to study in depth the Lincoln and, later, the Boone migrations and the intermarriages of the two families.

He graduated from high school in 1934, where he was a student of early American history. He worked his way through Mountain States College in Parkersburg, West Virginia and graduated in 1937 in business management. He followed this profession for the next forty-three years, retiring in 1980.

Mounts moved to Denver, Colorado, in 1944 where he was a scoutmaster for twenty-seven years. While associated with the scouts, other youth groups and community organizations, he received the Wood Badge in 1958 and the coveted Silver Beaver Award in 1965. For two years (1974-75), he was president of the Denver People-to-People/Sister City organization. During that time he accomplished the twinning of Denver with Nairobi, Kenya. He actively pursues the sports of fishing, golfing and skiing.

Mounts, a cinematographer for the past twenty-five years, has produced several 16mm travelogues covering two continents. He began research on the Boone and Lincoln families more than thirty-seven years ago and has been lecturing on the subject for several years.

Since 1979, he and his wife, Virginia, have traveled 92,000 miles, in their mobile trailer, in the United States, mostly doing research and photographing the many places where the Boone and Lincoln family members were born, lived, fought and died. He is honored to be the

468th recipient of the Lincoln Pilgrimage Certificate presented by the Lincoln National Life Foundation in Fort Wayne, Indiana.

This book is the outcome of his research, travel and five years of writing.   He hopes you derive as much pleasure reading this historical-biographical account of these famous families as he did putting it together.

Select Bibliography

Abraham Lincoln 1809-1959. Washington, D.C.: The Library of Congress in cooperation with the Lincoln Sesquicentennial Commission, 1959.

Appleman, Roy Edgar (editor). Abraham Lincoln--From His Own Words and Contemporary Accounts, Source Book Series 2. The National Park Service.

Barnes, Bertha. Daniel Boone. Modern Lith-Print Company, 1971.

Barrett, Joseph H. Life of Abraham Lincoln. Moore, Wilstach & Baldwin, 1865.

Beiting, Father Ralph W. Soldier of Revolution--A New View of Daniel Boone. Modern Lith-Print Company, 1977.

Bogart, W. H. Daniel Boone and the Hunters of Kentucky. Lee and Shepard, 1872.

Browne, F. F. The Every Day Life of Abraham Lincoln. N. D. Thompson Publishing Company, 1886.

Carnegie, Dale. Lincoln The Unknown. Carnegie & Associates, Inc., 1932 and 1959.

Elliott, Lawrence. The Legend That Was Daniel Boone. Reader's Digest Press, 1978.

Elliott, Lawrence. The Long Hunter--A New Life of Daniel Boone. Reader's Digest Press, 1976.

Hill, George Canning. Life of Daniel Boon--The Pioneer of Kentucky. Hovendon Company, 1859.

Lee. Eastern National Park & Monument Association, Source (Lattimore)

Book Series, No. 1. Produced by Colortone Press, 1964. Lincoln and the Lincoln Country. The Octavo Press. Lincoln, Waldo (editor). History of the Lincoln Family; Descendants of Samuel Lincoln 1637-1920. Boston; Goodspeed's Book Shop, Inc., 1981.

National Park Service. Daniel Boone--Thomas Walker. Cumberland Gap National Historical Park, Middlesboro, Kentucky.

Robert Todd Lincoln's Hildene. Vermont: Friends of Hildene, Inc.

Spaker, Hazel Atterbury (editor). The Boone Family. Baltimore; Genealogical Publishing Company, 1982.

Wagoner, Pat. The President's Mother--Nancy Hanks Lincoln. Keyprint, Inc., 1972. Wallace, Paul A. W.

Daniel Boone In Pennsylvania. Sponsored by the Commonwealth of Pennsylvania, Pennsylvania Historical and Museum Commission, 1971.

Weik, Jesse W. and William H. Herndon. Abraham Lincoln; The True Story of a Great Life. Vols. 1 and 2.

D. Appleton and Company, 1888 and 1892. "What Happened To Lincoln's Body?" In Life Magazine Vol. 54, No. 7. Time Inc., February 15, 1963.

Other Credits

Walter and Grace Stemme, Boone Monument Farm, Marthasville, MO.

Richard and Virginia Harris photo at Goosenest Prairie, IL.

Chicago Tribune Co, Chicago Historical Society, the McCutcheon Cartoon.

Lloyd Orendorf, several Lincoln photos, Dayton, OH.

Lincoln National Life Foundation, Ft. Wayne, Ind. Mark E. Neely, Jr., director. Ruth E. Cook, assistant director.

The Boone Family

George I
B England

George II
B Exeter
Devonshire,
England
D Age 60
M Sarah Uppey

George III Sr.
(1666-1744)
B Devonshire
Stoakes, England
D Berks Co., PA
M Mary Maugridge
(1669-1740
B Bradninch, England

George IV Jr.
(1690-1753)
B Bradninch, England
D Exeter, Berks Co. PA
M Debarah Howell
1713 (1691-1759)
Son William married
Sarah Lincoln

Sarah (1691-1744)
B Bradninch, England
M Jacob Stover 1715

Squire I (1696-1765)
B Bradninch, England
D Rowan Co., NC
M Sarah Morgan 1720
(1700-1777)
B Mocksville, NC (Both)

Mary (1699-1774)
B Bradninch, England
M John Webb 1720
B Berks Co., PA

John (1701-1785)
B Brandninch, England
D Exeter, Berks Co, PA
Dau. Ann married A.
Lincoln, son of
Mordecai II

Joseph (1740-1776)
B Bradninch, England
M Catherine (?)

Benjamin (1706-1762)
B Bradninch, England
M 1) Ann Farmer 1726
M 2 Susannah (?) 1736

James (1709-1785
B Bradninch, England
D Exeter, Berks Co. PA
M 1) Mary Foulke 1735
M 2) Ann Griffin 1757

Samuel (1711-1745)
B Bradninch, England
M Elizabeth Cassel 1734

Sarah (1724-1815)
B Bucks Co., PA
M John Wilcoxen 1742

Israel (1726-1776)
B Bucks Co., PA

Samuel (1728-1819)
B Bucks Co., PA
D Fayette Co., KY
M Sarah Day 1748

Johnathan (1730-1808)
B Exeter, Berks Co. PA
M Mary Carter

Elizabeth (1732-1825)
B Exeter, Berks Co. PA
D (? - ?) KY
M William Grant 1750

Daniel (1734-1820)
B Exeter, Berks Co. PA
D Defiance-St.Charles
County, MO
M Rebecca Bryan 1756
(1739-1813)
B 1) Marthasville, MO
B 2) Fankfort, KY

Mary (1736-1819)
B Exeter, Berks Co. PA
M William Bryan 1754
in Rowan Co., NC
(Uncle of Rebecca)

George (1739-1820)
B Exeter, Berks Co, PA
M Ann Linville 1764

Edward(Ned)(1740-80)
B Exeter, Berks Co. PA
M Martha Bryan
(Sister of Rebecca)
D Blue Licks, KY

Squire (1744-1815)
B Exeter, Berks Co. PA
D Corydon, IN
M Jane VanCleve 1765

Hanna (1746-1828)
B Exeter, Berks Co. PA
M1) John Stewart 1765
M2) Richard Pennington

James (1757-1773)
B Sugar Creek, NC
D Powell Valley, VA

Israel (1759-1782)
B Sugar Creek, NC
D Blue Licks, KY

Susannah (1760-1800)
B Culpeper, VA
D Defiance, MO
M William Hayes 1775
    (1754-1804)

Jemima * (1762-1829)
B Culpeper, VA
D Marthasville, MO
M Flanders Calloway
1782 (1758-1824)
M Boonesborough, KY

Levina (1766-1802)
B Sugar Creek, NC
D (?) KY
M Joseph Scholl 1785
    (1755-1835)

Rebecca (1768-1805)
B Brushey Mtn, NC
D Clark Co., KY
M Phil Goe 1767-1805

Daniel Morgan
(1769-1839)
B Beaver Creek, NC
D Jackson Co., MO
M Sarah G. Lewis 1800
    (1786-1850)

Jesse Bryan 1773-1820
B Beaver Creek, NC
D (?) MO
M Chloe Van Bibber
    (1772- ?)

William (1775-1775)
B Powell Valley, VA

Nathan (1781-1856)——
B Boone Station, KY
D Green Co., MO
M Olive Van Bibber
1799 (1783-1858)

* Note: Daniel's younger brother, Ned, was the father of Daniel's daughter Jemima.

Benjamin Howard
M Mary Stallard 1851
Green Co., MO

John Coburn
M Mary Wardlow

Levica
M William Cawlfield

Melvian (1820-1900)
M 1) James Howard
M 2) Franklin Frazier

Mary (1822-1915)
M Alfred Hosman 1841
At the time of her death, she was the last grandchild of Daniel and Rebecca Boone.

The Lincoln Family

Richard

Edward

Thomas I
(-1675)
B England
M 1 Susan
(-1641)
M 2 Mary
(-1683)

a
Samuel I ————
(1619-1690)
B Norwich, England
D Hingham, MA
M Martha Lyford
(-1693)
Came to America
in 1637

Samuel II (aa)
(1650-1720)
B Hingham, MA
M Debora Hersey

Daniel (ab)
(1652-1732)
B Hingham, MA
M Elizabeth Lincoln

Mordecai (ac)
(1655-1655)
B Hingham, MA

Mordecai I Sr. (ad) ————
(1657-1727)
B Hingham, MA
D Scituate, MA
M 1) Sarah Jones 1685
M 2) Mary Chapin 1701

Thomas (ae)
(1659-1661)
B Hingham, MA

Mary (af)
(1662-1752)
B Hingham, MA
M Joseph Bates

Thomas II (ag)
(1664-1715)
B Hingham, MA
M Mehitable Frost

Martha (ah)
(1666-1740)
B Hingham, MA

Sarah (ai)
(1669-1669)
B Hingham, MA

Sarah (aj)
(1671-1743)
B Hingham, MA

Rebecca (ak)
(1673-1757)
B Hingham, MA
M 1) John Clarke
M 2) Israel Nicholas

Mordecai II Jr. (ada) ————
(1686-1736)
B Hingham, MA
D Amity, PA, Berks Co.
M 1) Hanna Salter
M 2 Mary Robeson

Abraham (adb)
(1688-1745)
B Hingham, MA
M Rebecca

Issac I (adc)
(1691-1771)
B Hingham, MA
D Scituate, MA
M1) Sarah Cummings
M 2 Jael Garrett

Sarah (add)
(1694-1774)
B Scituate, MA
M Daniel Tower

Elizabeth (ade)
(1703-1724)
B Scituate, MA
M Ambrose Cole

Jacob I (adf)
(1708-1770)
B Scituate, MA
M 1) Mary Holbrook
M 2) Susanna Marbel

John I (Va. John) —————
(adaa) (1716-1788)
B Freehold, NJ
D Linville, VA
  Rockingham, CO.
M Rebecca Flowers
	Abraham I (Capt) —————
	(adaaa) (1744-1786)
	B Berks Co. PA
	D Jefferson Co.
	Eastwood, KY
	M Bathsheba Herring
	  at Linville Creek, VA
	1770 Rockingham, Co.
	(1745-1833)
	B Mill Creek, KY	

Debora (adab) (1717-1720) B Freehold, NJ		Mordecai IV (adaaa a) (1771-1830) B Rockingham Co. Linville Creek, VA D IL M Mary Mudd
Hannah (adac) (1720-1769) B Freehold, NJ M Joseph Millard	Hannah (adaab) (1748-1803) B Berks Co. PA M Robert Harrison	Josiah (adaaa b) (1773-1835) B Rockingham Co. Linville Creek, VA D IN M Catharine Barlow
Mary (adad) (1723-1769) B Freehold, NJ M Francis Yarnall	Lydia (adaac) (1748 - ?) B Berks Co. Pa M Bryan	Mary (adaaa c) (1775-1832) B Rockingham Co. Linville Creek, VA M Ralph Crum
Anne (adae) (1725-1812) B Freehold, NJ M William Tallman	Issac II (adaad) (1750-1816) B Berks Co. PA M Mary Ward	Thomas V (adaaa d)————— (1778-1851) B Rockingham Co. Linville Creek, VA D Coles Co., IL M 1) Nancy Hanks
Sarah (adaf) (1727-1810) B Exeter, PA Berks Co. M Willian Boone 1748	Jacob II (adaae) (1751-1822) B Berks Co. PA M Dorcas Robinson	1806 (1783-1818) M 2) Sarah Bush Johnston 1819 Elizabethtown, KY (1788-1869)
Mordecai III (adag) (1730-1812) B Exeter, PA Berks C0. M Mary Webb	John II (adaaf) (1755-1835) B Berks Co. PA M Mary Yarnell	Nancy (Ann) (adaaa e) (1780-1845) B Rockingham Co., VA Linville Creek, VA
Thomas III (adah) (1732-1775) B Exeter, PA Berks Co. M Elizabeth Davis	Sarah (adaag) (1757- ?) B Berks Co. PA M Dean	D Elizabethtown, KY M William Brumfield

Abraham (adai)
(1736-1806)
B Exeter, PA Berks Co.
M Ann Boone 1760
  (Daughter of James
  Boone)
	Thomas IV (adaah)
	(1761-1819)
	B Berks Co. PA
	D KY
	M Elizabeth Casner	

	Rebecca (adaai) (1767-1840) B Linville Creek, VA Rockingham Co. D Greenville, TN M John Rimel 1786	

Sarah (adaaa da)
(1807-1828)
B. Elizabethtown, KY
D Gentryville, IN
M Aaron Grigsby 1826

Abraham II (adaaa db)
(1809-1865)
B Hodgenville, KY
D Washington, DC
B Springfield, IL
M Mary Todd 1842
(1818-1882)
B Lexington, KY
D Springfield, IL

Thomas VI (adaaa dc)
(1812-1812)
B Knob Creek, KY
D Knob Creek, KY

Robert Todd
(adaaa dba)
(1843-1926)
B Springfield, IL
D Manchester, VT
Buried   Arlington
Cemetery, VA
M Mary Harlan 1868

Edward
(adaaa dbb)
(1846-1850)
B Springfield, IL
D Springfield, IL

William (Willie)
(adaaa dbc)
(1850-1862)
B Springfield, IL
D Washington, DC
B Springfield, IL

Thomas VII (Tad)
(adaaa dbd)
(1853-1871)
B Springfield, IL
D Chicago, IL
Buried Springfield, IL

Mary
(adaaa dbaa)
(1869-1938)
B Chicago, IL
D New York City
M Charles Isham in
    London,   England
1891 (1853- ?)

Abraham (Jack) III
(adaaa dbab)
(1873-1890)
D London, England
B1) Arlington Cemetery
B2) Oakridge Cemetery
1901

Jessie
(adaaa dbac)
(1875-1948)
D Rutland, VT
M 1) Warren Beckwith
    (1873-1955)
M Milwaukee, WI 1897
M 2) Frank Johnson
1915 (1873- ?)
M Manchester, VT
M3) Robert Randolp
  1926 (1873 - ?)
M Washington, DC

Lincoln Isham
(adaaa dbaaa)
(1892-1971)
B New York City
M Thelma Correa
(no children)

Mary Lincoln Beckwith
(adaaa dbaca)
(1898-1975)
B Mt. Pleasant, IA
(never married)

Robert Todd Lincoln
Beckwith
(adaaa dbacb)
(1904-1985)
B Riverside, IL
D Saluda, VA
M 1) Hazel Wilson
D 1964
(no children)
M 2) Annamarie
  Hoffman 1967
(no children)
Divorced 1976
M 3) Margaret Fristoe
1981 (no children)

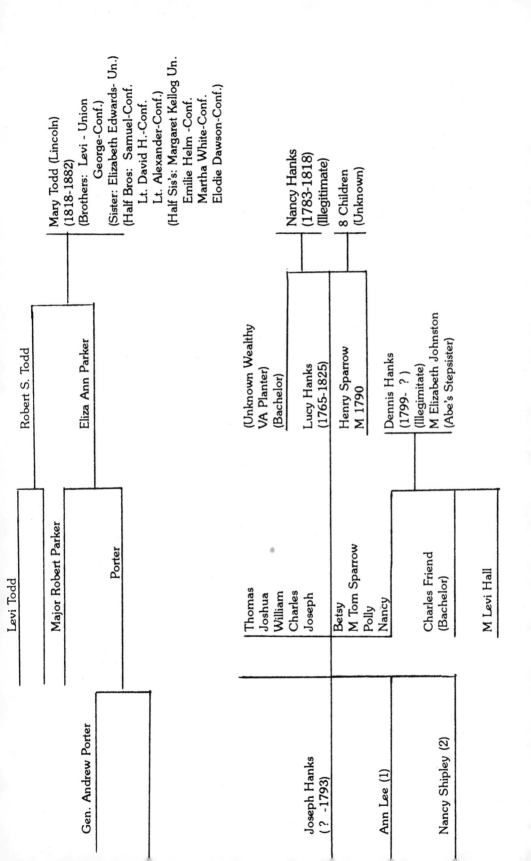

Levi Todd

Robert S. Todd

Mary Todd (Lincoln)
(1818-1882)
(Brothers: Levi - Union
George-Conf.)
(Sister: Elizabeth Edwards- Un.)
(Half Bros: Samuel-Conf.
Lt. David H.-Conf.
Lt. Alexander-Conf.)
(Half Sis's: Margaret Kellog Un.
Emilie Helm -Conf.
Martha White-Conf.
Elodie Dawson-Conf.)

Major Robert Parker

Eliza Ann Parker

Porter

Gen. Andrew Porter

Thomas
Joshua
William
Charles
Joseph

(Unknown Wealthy
VA Planter)
(Bachelor)

Nancy Hanks
(1783-1818)
(Illegitimate)

Lucy Hanks
(1765-1825)

8 Children
(Unknown)

Betsy
M Tom Sparrow
Polly
Nancy

Henry Sparrow
M 1790

Joseph Hanks
(? -1793)

Charles Friend
(Bachelor)

Dennis Hanks
(1799- ?)
(Illegitimate)
M Elizabeth Johnston
(Abe's Stepsister)

Ann Lee (1)

M Levi Hall

Nancy Shipley (2)

204

Index

ORDER FORM

THE PIONEER AND THE PRAIRIE LAWYER

Mail To:

Ginwill Publishing Company
2585 S. Holly Place – Dept. M2
Denver, CO   80222-6255

Enclose a check or money order.

Quantity _____ book(s) @ $14.95 each $ _____

Colorado residents add 3.8% sales tax $ _____

Shipping and Handling add $2.00 per book $ _____

                                    Total $ _____

                         Mailing Label

SHIP TO (please type or print):

Name: _____

Address: _____

City: _____ State: _____ Zip: _____